PRAISE FOR PREPARING FOR COLLEGE ADMISSIONS

"*Preparing for College Admissions* provides an excellent road map for parents and students to ensure that the higher education institution they finally select is the right one for them. You have laid out a thoughtful, step-by-step process to make sure that they not only make the right choice, but you have shown them how to pay for it as well. At every stage of the process, you have provided answers, discussed how to overcome hurdles and shown why this does not have to be a stress-filled exercise. After completing *Preparing for College Admissions*, you walk away knowing that the writer is extremely knowledgeable about the entire process, has lived it for years and has excelled in making it work for many families."

T. Eloise Foster
Secretary of the Maryland Department of Budget and Management

"*Preparing for College Admissions* is a practical, insightful guide that clarifies a very tedious and challenging process....how to prepare your child for college.

After twenty plus years as a Supervisor of School Guidance and having reviewed many college preparatory guides, magazines, books, etc., I can say with confidence that *Preparing for College Admissions* is a well-organized, excellent resource and should be in the hands of every parent and high school student."

Cynthia H. Beaver
Supervisor of School Guidance/Talented and Gifted Programs
New Haven Public Schools
New Haven, Connecticut

"In the array of guides available to students and parents, Carolyn's guide stands out because she speaks from the perspective of a highly successful counselor who has worked in K-12 schools and in higher education and has listened to and later helped thousands of parents and students, many of whom believed college was beyond their reach. She anticipates and answers the reader's questions in her engaging, often humorous, style. She also provides a candid behind-the-scenes look at critical matters such as financial aid.

Carolyn has devoted her life to helping urban students. My son, who is now in a physics Ph.D. program, was one of them. I am so pleased to see that her experience can now be shared with a larger audience."

Dr. Nancy Carriuolo
Deputy Commissioner for Higher Education and Chief Academic Officer
RI Office of Higher Education

"As a plethora of College Admissions Guides flood the market and promise success to hopeful students, few offer a more thought provoking and insightful book than *Preparing for College Admissions*. Baker's advice throughout is very sound. She packs 20 years of college counseling into one concise admissions guidebook with ease and a sense of humor. Her writing style is easy to follow, yet detailed enough to personalize the process. This is a must resource for parents and students that will make the college admission process more enjoyable and much more rewarding."

Donna Frederick-Neznek
Art Teacher

"*Preparing for College Admissions* will provide a rich resource to families at all stages of the college application process. Ms. Baker leads her readers through the labyrinth of college admissions with care and clarity, and her sensible, reassuring tone makes this journey seem not only manageable, but even fun. Both high-school students and their parents should welcome this detailed handbook as the perfect companion on the increasingly forbidding path to a college education."

Chloe Kitzinger
Yale University, Class 2006

"I was absorbed by the workbook style questions, which enable the student to think deeply about what his/her dreams are and how to accomplish them. This book gives specifics to students regarding what they should be doing in high school to help them achieve success in college. Professionally and accurately done!!!"

Jo Palmieri
Albert Schweitzer Institute

"*Preparing for College Admissions* exhibits knowledgeable care and concern, and provides many good and helpful suggestions, tips and ideas based on obvious experience. For those who are intimidated by or apprehensive about how to take on the whole college-prep and college-selection issue, this book is a hand-holding companion/guide/comforter to students and parents to proceed and succeed with confidence."

Atty. Don Bertrand

"Each year, it is more difficult for American families to get their children placed in the right college or university where thy can realize the ultimate dream of becoming all that they can be. The whole college admissions process can be overwhelming, negotiating increasing costs, entrance exams and other related obstacles to getting a good college education. *Preparing for College Admissions*, in a very pragmatic and interesting manner provides a well-designed road map for getting this job done efficiently and effectively. Buy this book, but most importantly, use it."

Loumis S. Taylor, MBA
Writer and Lecturer
Loumis@mris.com

"*Preparing for College Admissions* is an easy read. The author spells out everything for the student and parent. It is thorough and clear. Any parent who doesn't know the process will know exactly what to do after reading this book."

K. Saint John
Guidance Counselor

Preparing for
COLLEGE ADMISSIONS

The Ultimate Guide for Parents and Students

CAROLYN CROOM BAKER

Preparing for College Admissions

CAROLYN CROOM BAKER

© Carolyn Croom Baker 2006

Published by 1stWorld Publishing
1100 North 4th St. Fairfield, Iowa 52556
tel: 641-209-5000 • fax: 641-209-3001
web: www.1stworldpublishing.com

First Edition

LCCN: 2006939915

SoftCover ISBN: 978-1-4218-9916-9

eBook ISBN: 978-1-4218-9917-6

This material has been written and published solely for educational purposes. The author and the publisher shall have neither liability nor responsibility to any person or entity with respect to any loss, damage or injury caused or alleged to be caused directly or indirectly by the information contained in this book.

The characters and events described in this text are intended to entertain and teach rather than present an exact factual history of real people or events.

Table of Contents

ACKNOWLEDGEMENTS

God blesses us through other people. I have been blessed to have some extraordinary people in my life who have encouraged and supported me through the process of writing *Preparing for College Admissions*.

To my parents Asa and Clara Croom, my eternal gratitude for making books, writing, and faith a major part of my childhood and for nurturing those interests into later years.

Sondra Jordan, you have been an important part of my life for decades. Your encouragement, friendship, editorial suggestions, pushing, and frequent motivational talks kept me focused on the project and helped me to bring it to completion. Your energy is contagious.

My angelic team of readers, Cynthia Beaver, Eloise Foster, Sue White, Brenda Jones, Lois Strayhorn, Loumis Taylor, Arlene Baker, Shawna Strayhorn, Karen Saint John, Cari Strand, Jo Palmieri, Donald Bertrand, Nancy Carriuolo, Troy Tate, and Donna Frederick-Neznek patiently gave invaluable advice and counsel. Cynthia, I thank you for your daily support, generosity, true friendship, and kindness. Your wisdom is priceless. Eloise, I thank you for your patience, editorial suggestions, attention to the project, and lasting friendship. Sue, your constant enthusiasm for my work, emotional support, sense of humor, and advice are treasures I will always value. Brenda, your sense of form, style, and good judgment are qualities I admire. Thank you for sharing them with me. You were always there to listen, to motivate, and to encourage perseverance. Lois and Shawna, you are great examples of how to do college admissions the right way. Loumis, your careful read and business advice gave me help at a time when it was needed. Karen and Donna, thank you for taking the time to support my goal even in the midst of your own work. Arlene, I deeply appreciate your advice, concern, and editorial suggestions. Thanks for insisting that I follow the rules. Cari, please know how much I appreciate your attention and careful reading at the end of the project. To Gita, my editor, thank you for your conscientious attention to detail and gentle support. Jo and Troy, thank you for making a place for my work in your hectic schedule. Your comments and suggestions were so helpful to me. Nancy, thank you for being there at the final hour and for your advice, support, and encouragement.

Carl Baker, thank you for your encouragement and a constant belief in my goals. You have always supported my creative journey and for that, I am grateful.

To all of the guidance counselors, graduate students, college admissions officers, and school administrators with whom I have had the pleasure to work, thank you for sharing your insights, questions, concerns, and wisdom. My own professional development was enriched because of you.

Finally, to all of the parents and students who trusted me with their goals, intentions, and ambitions, thank you. I learned as much from you as you learned from me. It has always been my honor to serve you.

Carolyn Croom Baker

Dear Parents and Students,

In over 20 years as a College Placement Consultant, I have coached more than 5,000 parents and students through the college admissions process and into the nation's best colleges and universities, schools that educate while building character.

During that time, it was my honor to meet and exchange ideas with hundreds of college admissions officers. They shared the questions they heard from families most often and how they resolved them. I, too, listened carefully to the questions from parents and students and found common concerns. Parents and students worried about campus lifestyles and values, choosing a major that would provide a satisfying future, how to continue a practice of family values while living away from home, and campus safety. They also worried about how to turn high school experiences into college success.

The biggest family concern has always been about money; how do parents find the money to pay for a college education without sacrificing the family lifestyle or mortgaging the house. I have advised families who worried because they had no money and no house to mortgage and wealthy families who wanted to find a way to conserve some of their savings for their child's life after college. I have coached independent students who had no parents and had to handle their education alone. Trust me. I have heard almost everything. Yet, I can say with confidence that there is a perfect college or university for every child who wants a college education, and there is definitely plenty of money to pay for it, and not just loans.

Bottom-line—students who follow this system will secure more than enough money to cover college costs.

My work with students and families has been truly rewarding. I hear from students regularly who tell me about their successful lifestyles and how much they appreciate having received an education that made them leaders and gave them strong character. Student and parent comments prompted me to put the concerns that they raised most often and the solutions into one book.

This guide was written to help students and parents position themselves to access the best education possible by knowing how to secure college admissions, college financing, and college success. Now instead of a few hundred families per year, I can teach thousands these strategies. I wish you extraordinary success on this journey.

Carolyn Croom Baker, M.A., M.Ed.
National Certified Counselor

INTRODUCTION

Preparing for College Admissions is about success. Your success. This is a book for future leaders, young people who have ambition, and for parents who are ready to help their children get the best college education possible. *Preparing for College Admissions* answers two questions:

> • **How will you prepare for, select, apply, and get admitted to a college that will provide an excellent education, honor family values, and develop your character?**

> • **Where will you find the money to pay for a college like this?**

Tomorrow's leaders will have to be smart. They will also need strong character, conviction, vision, and a sense of purpose to conquer 21st century challenges. The right college will teach its students well and help them to evolve into creative problem solvers who base their decisions on the highest ethical standards.

Parents and students start out expecting to find the college that will be the right match. They hope for extraordinary character building experiences and the money to cover all expenses. Yet, somewhere in the process, a lot of students end up in the wrong place and never get a college degree.

Only 59% of college freshmen actually graduate from the college in which they initially

enrolled, according to a U.S. Government Accounting Office report. Forty-one percent either transfer to another school or drop out. That means that only a little more than half of the expected freshman class will receive a college degree within six years. The other half will either begin again at another college or drop out of college altogether. That is money wasted, dreams deferred.

Parents and students, you must be diligent and look deeply at college choices and the reasons for the choice. If you don't ask the right questions, you will never get the right answers, and that leads to poor placement, which puts good students at risk for not completing college.

Parents invest a lot of time and energy to help young people build character strength on the way to adulthood. The right college will continue that work and build intellectual muscle. The college years are perfect for analyzing, refining, and strengthening character. It is the time when students, away from parents and everything familiar, must rely on their own personal compasses to determine choices.

In the face of current challenges to society's previously accepted moral values, college must do more than provide a diploma, a skill set, or academic mastery. It must create environments for probing values and helping students to develop personal ethical standards. The right college provides multiple, consistent opportunities to reflect on, examine, and practice building and strengthening character.

Preparing for College Admissions puts parents and students in control and teaches you when, where, how, and under what conditions to start and manage the college admissions process. The prize does not go to the one who simply works hard, does well, scores well, and follows all the rules. The prize, admission to the best college for each student, goes to the one who works the plan the right way at the right time.

Read this book, if you want to know:

- **How to choose the college that is the right fit for you.**

- **How to select a college that builds character and supports values.**

- **Where to find scholarships and how to secure them.**

- **How to get financial aid.**

- **What college entrance exams to take and when to take them.**

- **How extracurricular activities can lead to scholarships.**

- **How to set up a mastermind team of allies to support your goals.**

- **How to package a winning college application.**

- **Tips for a successful college interview.**

- **Which high school courses lead to success.**

- **How to stay safe in a changing world.**

- **How to use the Internet to select colleges and locate scholarships.**

Preparing for College Admissions clarifies and demystifies the unknown components of the college admissions process and leaves you and your family with a quiet sense of well being, knowing that you have done the best for your child's future.

Preparing for College Admissions shows parents and students, in simple steps, how to select the school that is the best match. With almost 4,000 colleges and universities in this country, that can be a daunting task—and that number does not include the community colleges and other two-year institutions. In this book, you will learn how to whittle that number down to seven or eight perfect schools. You will learn how to select schools that will continue the job you started all those short years ago, colleges that will support and expand on the values you and your family hold dear while providing an education that will make you proud. Students, you will learn how to find that school where you will truly feel at home; where there are more people who share your values than not; where you can find full expression for your special talents, build wonderful memories, make lasting friendships, and develop the gifts that you and only you can bring to the world. In this book, you learn how to define your values and goals and make them clear to others.

Early starters learn how to manage their high school careers to become prime candidates for America's best colleges. They will have a major advantage over the competition. Late starters learn how to maximize current opportunities and end up on the right track, right up front where they will be noticed. Whether you start early or late or just somewhere in the middle, *Preparing for College Admissions* provides guidelines that lead to success.

By mid-senior year, both parents and students will be able to celebrate the college admission decision. The best thing about it all is that everything will happen without stress, anxiety, or one moment of headache. When your friends ask why you look so calm, you will simply smile and know that everything is under control. Better yet, you will save the thousands of dollars many college placement gurus charge for their services.

It is true that some families should work with an independent college placement consultant. Some parents just can't make the time, work away from home, or are just too overwhelmed by life's other pressures to handle college admissions themselves. However, the good news is that most families can easily work this program, save a lot of money, and enjoy the process. Besides, it is a wonderful opportunity for parents and students to create a lasting memory while working through a life-changing question. It may be the last time that parents and their children have the chance to give this kind of attention to each other's needs. Relish the moments, hours, and days together. You can never recapture them.

Young people can sometimes seem aloof or like they are moving in some sort of complex choreography between the adult world and their own. They may not say it, but young people both need and appreciate their parents' counsel and involvement as they make major choices.

Parents

When your neighbor or office mate asks you what the fuss is all about and advises you to just send your child to the local college whether it is a fit or not and call it a day, you can tell them why you are taking such care to send your child to college the right way. You can tell them that college frequently determines life-long friends, who one marries, career track, income potential, and future home, along with personality and character development. You want your child to be in a position to access the best and become the best.

There are colleges in the United States that will meet every personal, social, and academic need, colleges that will help your child grow into an accomplished, self-fulfilled adult. But the news gets better. There are financial aid programs and scholarships to fit every circumstance and every need. **With hard work and a simple system, good students can actually go to college for free.** Finding the right college in the right way is essential to your child's future happiness. Finding it at the right price is certain to enhance yours. In this book, you will learn how to guide your child into an awesome college experience and how to find the money to pay for it. **I have helped thousands of young people get the best deal of their lifetime: a free college education.**

Student

You are about to embark on the greatest adventure of your life. The decisions that you make at this time can enrich you, change you, or do both. They can take you into previously unconsidered directions, where you will meet new people and travel to places that were once fantasies. You are about to choose a new home. There is nothing more exciting and potentially rewarding than creating for one's self a new life with new experiences in a brand new place in a brand new way.

When you graduate from college, you will want to know that you can stand firmly on your own, comfortable with your choices, and secure in the person that you will have become. **The right college will teach you how to survive in a complex world, how to live with honor, how to assess risk, and how to embrace life.**

Before getting started, choose a set of colored pencils. I encourage you to record feelings, impressions, wisdom moments, and special memories. You will evolve in this process, and later, you will appreciate a record of the journey. **In this case, it is the journey and the destination that matters.**

1

HOW TO USE THIS GUIDE

Throughout the book, I address some comments to parents and others to students. However, the book can help best if parents and students read it all and discuss it together.

There is space in this book for students to write answers to questions and clarify ideas. Write your answers in pencil just in case you want to make changes and you probably will as you complete this process (I love making entries like that with colored pencils). Take your time and complete them carefully. The work that you do will help you sharpen your focus and ultimately get you into the right college. If you need more space to answer questions than I provide, a journal is a great place to write. You may have other questions that you would like to answer. Feel free to write those questions down, and after your research, write in the answers.

If you are like me, you will be tempted to read the book from beginning to end before completing any of the assignments. You might even think that you can do the assignments mentally, and with a few short notes, complete the task. Resist that temptation. Writing is a powerful activity. When you put your goals and ideals on paper and take time to examine them, you have the opportunity to clarify ideals and bring dreams closer to reality. Somehow, the process of writing your goals, ideals, or intentions makes you more accountable for making them happen.

While writing, you may wish to share what you write with friends or family. You can do that, and sometimes input from those who know and love you can be helpful. Ultimately, you will have to answer all questions according to your beliefs and values.

When you finish reading this book, you will find a list of resources. Use them and add others to the list. There are books that you should read and Web sites to check out. Be sure to call your state office of higher education for information about state-sponsored programs.

Take your time and cover all topics completely. Consider this book your private college placement consultant.

2

BEGINNINGS

Parents

It seems like only a few years ago that you took your child to school for the first time. You remember it like it was yesterday. Where did the time go? Well, it slipped by while you were raising your child in the best way that you knew how. It slipped by while you were taking your son to soccer and your daughter to gymnastics. Or was it music? It slipped by while you were baking brownies, planning Sunday dinners, hosting sleepovers, finding tutors, organizing homework, going to school meetings, managing your home and your life. Well actually, your life and your child's life were the same. And now, here you stand, you and your child, just at the beginning of another life-changing event. You will take your child to school once more for the first time, but this time will be different. This time your daughter will return as a woman and your son as a man.

You may think that you're not ready for this. Your child may even think that he or she is not ready. You are. Your child is. You've done your job well. You taught your child good values. You raised him or her with love. You taught your child about discipline, organization, caring for others, and the power of service. You taught them to trust their instincts, to be honest, and to have integrity. You taught them about faith in God and faith in self. You gave them the courage and the permission to explore and to seek knowledge. You encouraged intellectual curiosity. You taught them when to be leaders and when to follow, and to reach for opportunities to express all of their talents. You are ready.

Your son understands now why you insisted he always do his best and why you continued to encourage his participation in student government. Your daughter understands now why you never accepted less than her best and why you encouraged each new initiative and school project. Now, your child understands the reasons for all of the hard work and discipline. Your child is ready.

There are children who did not learn their lessons well. Some families had difficult times and some children had years that are tough to explain. People understand that. You will soon learn that college admissions people are some of the most understanding. So don't throw up your hands because your child made mistakes along the way. There are places on the college application and in the college essay where students may explain a difficult personal history.

If your child is brilliant, mature, talented beyond measure, and every college in America is beating a path to your door, consider yourself blessed. Your task is not as complex. Opportunities will probably fall into your child's lap. Unfortunately, only about 5 percent of students fall into that highly sought-after category. Everyone else will need help to reach his or her goal, and that is what this book offers.

The drama begins in eighth or ninth grade when school guidance counselors initiate conversations about schedules and courses for students on the fast track, courses that will get smart students into smart colleges. At this point, parents learn that they have to get more involved in the decision-making process, more involved in the school. There are now more meetings, more college fairs, and more parent workshops. Rumors about how to get students into top schools run rampant through your neighborhood. The anxiety surrounding the college admissions process can be suffocating. Rumors about secret connections to admissions offices, SAT coaching with magical results, and scholarships to be had with just a phone call from the right person are pervasive. There is one rumor that is easier to believe than all of the others. You have probably heard it:

> *Your child's school is high on the college recruiters' radar screens because they know only the best and the brightest students attend there. The constant flow of recruiters will give your child an edge over students at other schools that recruiters don't visit and will assure him or her a place in a top-tier college.*

How many parents all across America are making their plans based on that same rumor? College admissions officers visit most high schools by the way. They know there are great students in every school.

O.K. You think you have it all under control. You say you can handle this. So, why all the Excedrin and chipped fingernails? After all, you raised wonderful children. They've done well in school. You gave them honorable values like honesty, justice, service, and tolerance for differences. You've taught them great problem-solving skills, gotten them passionately involved in the politics of their community, shown them the power of service, and taught them social responsibility. Now, thanks to you, they also have a spiritual practice that makes you proud. This year, your second child enters high school.

Then imagine one night you hear your daughter say:

> *Mom, Dad, I'm going to be a research scientist. Today, in science class, we talked about a project that works to preserve vegetation in the Amazon jungle. My teacher said that there are plants and herbs that can heal many diseases. Can you imagine that? And these plants are at risk. Scientists are needed to research and harvest them for more study. I have to do this kind of work. I need to make a difference in the world. I know I'm only in the ninth grade, but some of my friends are already talking about college. We've got to make plans.*

"Sure, of course", *you say.*

You notice that your husband is quiet. Then your son pipes in. He's sure now. He has decided not to tour with his band even though he's the lead singer and guitarist. He is going to college, and he wants to be a politician. He recognizes the need to express his many talents. He wants to help make society better. He has great ideas, he tells you. He was born to lead, but he never wants to lose his connection to music. After all, he has seen other successful politicians display their musical talents. Why not him? Your son is a high school junior.

"Music is in my soul", he chants as he leaves the room with his sister for home-work, computer chat, telephone calls, secret teenage rituals, or whatever.

You look at your husband. Is that a wrinkle on his brow? Did you just feel your stomach quiver? No. Absolutely not. After all, your husband is a well-educated lawyer, and you teach the fifth grade at a very prestigious middle school. Although it was twenty years ago, you both have had experience with applying to college. You're certain that you know enough to set your child on the right path. Your husband is still quiet. He heads for the den to watch a soccer game, but makes no comment. The next day, you drive to a bookstore just to see what books are available about the SAT and getting ready for college, just in case there've been some slight adjustments in the last two decades. You are certain there've been a few changes but not too many.

When the nice salesperson leads you to the right section of the store, you are shocked. There are shelves and shelves of books on college readiness and admissions to the right school and ten more shelves on the SAT. Then there's the ACT (American College Test), another college entrance exam. You flip through a few books. "What is all of this?" you think. You discover that the SAT has changed some in twenty years. Actually, it has changed a lot. Sixteen hundred is no longer the winning ticket. Twenty-four hundred is now the perfect score. Achievement Tests have now become SAT Subject Tests, and there are so many of them. The math questions seem more difficult, and then, there's the new writing test.

"When did that happen?" you wonder. "When did college entry get so competitive, so complicated"?

You know you have neither the time nor the desire to muddle through all of these books and study guides. It's not that you don't care. It's not that you wouldn't make any investment of time or money, move any obstacle just to make your children happy and their futures bright. It's not that at all. To tell the real truth, it's confidence. What if you don't get it right? Are you starting to feel like a fish out of water?

Your children are so involved with schoolwork, clubs, church, and friends; and then there is your son's band and your daughter's dance team. Somehow, you don't remember being that busy when you were in high school. It seemed as if your parents had more time for you, or was that just your imagination? Has the world really changed that much in twenty years?

You have a solution. Tomorrow, you'll make an appointment with your children's guidance counselor, who you are sure knows them well and can take you through this labyrinth without a scratch, and you'll preserve order at home. You'll tell the guidance counselor about your family's values and that character development is just as important to you as academic prowess. You'll let him know that you are looking for a great school that will continue to nurture the values that have been the foundation of your family. He'll understand and know exactly what to do. The problem is settled, or so you think.

At dinner, you explain your plan. Your son announces in that all too familiar— "I am so in touch and you are so out of it"—voice that you already have an appointment with the guidance counselor. Everyone has them, and you will be getting something in the mail. He checks his planner for the date. "That's right," he says. It's May 17, 11:30 a.m. to noon for him and May 23, 1:30 p.m. to 2:00 p.m. for your daughter. It is now September. You want advice now. You want to be on track now.

Your daughter tells you that her best friend's mom has everything outlined and that Tricia (your daughter's best friend) will definitely get into one of the better colleges and become a super rich and even more beautiful genius member of society. Because Tricia's mom has it all together for her, Tricia will meet all of the right people who can guarantee that she'll lead the lifestyle of the rich and famous.

You all know a mom like Tricia's. Your daughter has mentioned her to you. You met her at the last PTA meeting. She's the one who always has time to head up the cookie drive. She does that even though she has three children, two dogs, and a cat. You've heard about how she gets up every morning at 5:00 am, throws three loads of clothes into the washer, while doing an hour on the tread-mill at full speed, then shampoos and blow-dries her hair, walks the dogs, feeds the cat, and prepares a sumptuous hot breakfast for her brood all before 7:00 am. She's a civic leader, volunteers for several charities including Tricia's school which is your child's school, and always looks like a fashion model even when she's coming back from the gym. Each morning she makes one more To Do list. She has one on the fridge, one on the dash of her car, and one in her purse. But Tricia's mom doesn't work twenty-two miles from home. In fact, Tricia's mom doesn't work outside of the home. You do.

When will you or your husband have time to take care of all of this college admissions business? And even if you could figure out how to make the time, what should you do first? Right now, you feel like a mouse in a maze. Which way do you go now, and just where is that bell? Are you getting the picture?

Yes, everything really has changed since you sent your two-page application off to college with a $20 application fee. By the way, the fee has changed, too. When you were a senior, your guidance counselor wrote a short recommendation, sent the transcript and your SAT's off to the admissions office, and all was well and done. Welcome to the twenty-first century and the new and improved world of college admissions where nothing is simple.

The college placement experts would like you to think that you're in way over your head, that you are about to ruin everything fumbling around on your own. Besides, you're not Tricia's mom. You've never been that organized and you've always hated all those To Do lists. You have strong networks and good contacts, you think, but not like Tricia's mom.

Your child's future is at stake, the experts say. They also tell you that if you want to assure your progeny at least a moderate chance for a successful future, you will need an outside consultant, someone outside of the local school, that is.

Just how much individual attention can the school guidance counselor give your child? Your child's counselor may work with as many as 200 students. Some guidance counselors have caseloads even larger than that. To be realistic, even in some of the best schools, where the caseload is one hundred or less, students still do not get as much individual attention as they may need.

Many guidance counselors are highly skilled, well informed, and totally dedicated to the process. Some high school administrators fully understand what it takes to make this whole thing work and provide support for the guidance office. Others may not. Most guidance counselors will work to make sure that they recommend colleges that prepare your child for adulthood by educating them and reinforcing their natural gifts. Some will just not be able to help with that. You must educate yourself so that you are in a better position to take charge and manage the process.

3

CHARACTER AND PURPOSE

Parents

There are important family values that you, your spouse, and your parents worked hard to instill in your children. How can you be sure that those values will not be lost on some fast-paced college campus? You've read, *"If you raise your children in the way that they should go, when they are old, they will not depart from it."* You've also read the newspapers and watched the evening news full of stories about young people on college campuses marching to a beat that you have never heard, and you hope your child finds a different tune altogether.

Does graduation from high school make your child an adult, or is there still more work to do? Perhaps they could use a few more years to hone their natural talents, unearth their vital gifts, and begin the lifelong process of uncovering purpose. The right campus can help them.

You make tremendous investments in your children as you prepare them for the adult world. The right college experience will allow your child to make the kind of smooth transition from childhood to adulthood that will make you proud and your child secure.

Student

Character strength is something that can be learned and upon which we can improve. Choices and experiences develop our character. Experiences that are rich with leadership, service, intellectual achievement, and ethical choices build character. Some colleges do an excellent job of exposing students to character-building activities. Others ignore the issue. You can't afford to ignore it.

When considering college placement, look beyond the obvious. Don't be seduced by designer labels. You are preparing for a life-changing experience. This is the time to lay the foundation for your greatest vision of yourself. The right college will help you accomplish that and more.

Newspapers are full of stories about leaders in business, government, and spiritual vocations who seem to be having a crisis of character. These are men and women who have reached the pinnacle of their careers; yet they parade across your television news screens each evening with complex tales of bad choices, unsavory motivations, and all manner of willful acts without conscience. Many of these people started out much like you are today, with a clean slate and a golden future. Many of them had parents, who loved, cared for, and nurtured their best qualities. So, what happened?

Strength of character is the foundation upon which everything we do stands. Character gives us the courage to make the right decisions even in the face of adversity. It makes it possible to pursue goals relentlessly during the times when rewards seem distant, and it gives our conscience a place in the forefront of life.

The college's role in strengthening character is pivotal. Some colleges are like an oasis of character-building opportunities. Others offer much less. Some students have the capacity to find wonderful opportunities for personal growth in the middle of a candy store. Students like this are naturally outgoing assertive go-getters. They are the ones who can create service projects where there are none and are not afraid to go against the tide of the popular and accepted.

Students with highly developed personal strength do not mind explaining themselves to others. They welcome it and do not mind in the least if others disagree or don't understand, as long as they believe that they are following the right path. Most students are not that strong. Most students leave high school still needing more nurturing and more character-building opportunities before evolving into their best person.

A college degree opens many doors and completion of graduate school opens even more. Yet, we all know people, young vibrant people, who have all of the right degrees but no personal fulfillment. Just look at the lists of best selling non-fiction books. Books about how to live a better, fuller, more meaningful life are always among the top. These "how to" books are most popular with the thirty-forty-something group. We're realizing that getting and getting more is not enough to guarantee a happy or personally satisfying life. These how-to books attempt to help us redesign our life's plan. There's an urge to rediscover natural talents, pursue long buried passions, and simply live a life more consistent with personal values.

What if we had gotten the design right at twenty or twenty-one? O.K., maybe that's a little unrealistic. Only the lucky few get it right at such an early age. Most don't. Yet, many of us would have come a lot closer to the best version of ourselves if we had been in an environment that nurtured personal growth and introspection. What if college could have played a more pivotal role in helping us discover what really matters in life? Better still, what if college could also have helped us to uncover purpose?

Recently, questions about life purpose have come to the forefront. Middle-aged people are still searching for a reason for being. The question that they ask is ancient. It goes something like, *"Why are we here on this planet at this time, and what are we supposed to be doing?"* The answer is one that we can all figure out if given the time and the support to do so. The process of uncovering our own personal answers will open the door to a more satisfying life. The answers will reveal our purpose.

Rewarding service experiences, occasions for creative expression, and opportunities to stretch beyond one's comfort zone can provide a path to uncovering purpose while building character and strength. I think the two go hand in hand. While we are involved in activities that strengthen character, purpose is revealed. The right college can put you on a solid path to both.

While preparing this section for you, I discovered a little magazine with a powerful message. Robert Roberts writes in *Logos Magazine*, "Character is greater and higher than money, intellect, or love—because it determines the use and direction of these three. It is the character of the rich man which determines whether he shall be a benefactor or a curse. It is character which determines whether the learned man shall use his knowledge as a destructive or a constructive force in society. It is character which determines whether love shall be a passion-working havoc in human life, or a grace beautifying and ennobling life. Character is the determining force behind money, talent, and love." (R. Roberts, Logos, Vol. 72, No. 9, pg. 425, June 2006.)

Next is a set of questions to help you think more about your character and purpose. Well thought out answers will help you define the person you intend to become. The right college will help you to evolve into that person.

DEFINING MY BEST SELF

I intend to be a _____**person.** (From this moment forward, what you intend to be or do will be the standard of excellence you will use as a model to live by.)

1. What would a _____person be like? Write down anything that comes to mind. Don't censor your thoughts.

_____

_____

_____

_____

2. What kind of personal environment would a _____ person have?

_____

_____

_____

3. How would a _____person display self-esteem/self worth?_____

_____

_____

_____

4. What kind of activities would attract a _____person and what role would a _____person play in those activities?

_____

Carolyn Croom Baker

_____

_____

_____

5. What kind of friends would a _____ person attract?

_____

_____

PERSONAL QUALITIES TO MAKE YOUR INTENTIONS REAL

Qualities

(Specific qualities I can nurture. Example: independence, courage, wisdom)

Actions

(Specific ways to make qualities prominent In my life)

_____   _____

_____   _____

_____   _____

_____   _____

_____   _____

_____   _____

_____   _____

_____   _____

LET YOUR INTENTION GUIDE YOUR DAILY ACTIVITIES

Review the actions list on the previous page. List at least five specific ways that show how you are already incorporating your intention in your activities.

1._____

_____

2._____

_____

3._____

_____

4._____

_____

5._____

_____

Now list at least five additional ways you could apply your intention to your activities. Remember that what you do from now on will be directed by your intention for your life.

1._____

_____

2._____

_____

3._____

_____

4._____

_____

5._____

_____

SPECIAL NOTES ABOUT YOUR INTENTIONS FOR THE KIND OF PERSON YOU PLAN TO BE.

_____
_____
_____
_____
_____
_____
_____
_____
_____
_____
_____
_____

4

YOUR VISION OF SUCCESS

Parents

When beginning any new project, careful planning makes everything easier, more organized, and less stressful. It also instills confidence that you are doing the right things just when you should be doing them. This book teaches you what to do and when to do the important tasks that will put your child into the college of your collective dreams.

You and your child are going to plan an academic course of study, extracurricular activities, civic projects, internships, and service projects with an end in mind. You know what you want for your family, so if you keep that desire in focus, planning and executing the plans will be much easier. When you take responsibility for important tasks, and you plan the specific actions for accomplishing those tasks, you are being proactive. If you sit back and wait for others to act first, you can only react to circumstances. You are smarter than that.

Before writing the details of the plan, we will spend some time in this chapter clarifying a vision of the perfect college education at the perfect school. Once that vision is clear, then we will know where to go.

Student

Start with a winner's attitude.

Some students don't have to work hard at that. Some students start this life with everyone in their world affirming their success and special qualities. Students who have always received straight A's, great test scores, and great leadership roles don't have to worry about creating an attitude for success. But there are others who have not been so fortunate. These students may just be a little shy, or have to study harder just to get C's and B's, or have to work a little harder on social skills, getting noticed, or being respected for natural talents.

Any new vision begins in the mind first before it manifests in the outer world. All of us have the power to change, at any moment, our current vision of who we are and to create a new one; and it starts with a single word. That word will come from the imagination.

Refer to your statements about your intention in the previous chapter. Your intention will form and direct your vision for your education. A great education is a foundation for a great life.

Commit to that vision now by putting it on paper. Describe the college life that you'd like to have. Give free rein to your imagination. Have fun with this. Just describe what you see in your vision for your college education. It doesn't matter what kind of life you have in high school. You have the power to create a new life experience. You will be amazed at the power in this exercise.

Step 1: DESCRIBE THE VISION IN DETAIL. GIVE IT LIFE.

1. What kind of day is it when you enter the college of your dreams? What does the campus look like, feel like?

_____

_____

_____

_____

2. What activities immediately appeal to you, and what role will you have in those activities?

_____

_____

_____

_____

3. What types of people do you attract?

_____

_____

_____

_____

4. What talents do you express?

_____

_____

_____

_____

5. Why do people appreciate you?

_____

_____

_____

_____

6. What are you wearing?

_____

_____

_____

_____

7. What is your room like?

_____

_____

_____

_____

8. What needs do you see in your new campus community that you will fill?

_____

_____

_____

_____

9. What will you study?

_____

_____

_____

_____

10. What do you do on campus that makes you proud?

_____

_____

_____

_____

If you've answered all of these questions, you now have the beginning of a vision statement, and that is all you need to get started. You can revise your vision as often as you like, as you grow into the greatness of who you really are.

Step 2: NOW, IN TWO SENTENCES OR LESS, WRITE A PRESENT TENSE STATEMENT OF THE LIFE AND CAMPUS EXPERIENCE THAT YOU INTEND TO HAVE.

One of these statements will become your college affirmation.

For example, you might say:

"I am so excited about my new campus home where I am a valued member of the community."

"While studying music in college I develop my natural talent and become the musician I always wanted to be. I am a valued member

of the campus music community."

"I participate in activities that I never considered before and I excel".

"I am meeting so many students who are smart and share my values. I enjoy and excel in every class."

Now you try it. Write a positive, present tense statement about your ideal experience at your ideal college.

My campus experience is

_____
_____
_____
_____
_____

Or

I am

_____
_____
_____
_____.

You could create so many other positive statements. Affirmations can keep you focused through the difficult times in high school. Just keep writing until you have a full paragraph or two that describes your future reality on a college campus. Be bold. Let it represent your grandest thoughts about you. You will not have to execute the plan alone. You will have allies. Keep it handy and read it often. It can also keep you moving forward through the college years.

Step 3: GATHER YOUR ALLIES

You can accomplish a lot on your own, but you can achieve even more with the help of others. You have resources in your hometown that can be a great asset to you. Keep your eyes and ears open for all of the many wonderful opportunities.

Allies on the radio

Sharpen your auditory skills. Don't just listen to the music and the beat. The radio is a great source for scholarships and college readiness opportunities. Most radio stations consider it their responsibility to the community to announce scholarship opportunities, college fairs, financial aid fairs, and scholarship information meetings. They promote all kinds of events that are designed to help you, like college open houses and bus tours to area colleges.

For all of you aspiring journalists, the Broadcast Journalist Association offers a scholarship each year to future journalists via the radio, but you have to be tuned in and listening for opportunities to hear them. In addition, individual philanthropists frequently use the radio to announce grants and scholarships. So, listen up!

Allies in the Print News Media

The local newspaper can also be one of your allies. Philanthropists often post grants, scholarships, and internship opportunities in the newspaper. Local civic organizations generally notify the high schools about scholarship opportunities that they fund, but they also put notices in the newspaper. You could be one of the first to know about a funding source that others might miss. Reporters will also write stories about opportunities that local civic groups provide. Some civic groups avoid notifying the schools simply because they may not know how to navigate school bureaucracy. Other civic groups may not trust school personnel to distribute the information fairly. They depend on the public media to get the word out. With so much homework and so many school activities, it may be hard to read the entire newspaper each day, but you can always skim the paper for information that will be important to you.

You should learn the layout of your local newspaper. The first section is generally big news stories, including stories of national interest. However, there are often pages in the very beginning of the paper where you can find **public service announcements**. If you don't know where these announcements are located in the paper, call the paper's main office and ask. The school librarian or the reference librarian at the local public library can also help with this. Most public service announcements will be short, only a paragraph or two, just to let people know about an event, service, or opportunity. They should be easy to find, once you know where to look.

Even the business section of the newspaper can be helpful. Sometimes corporate entities offer free money, scholarships, competitions, and internships for students and announce it in the business section of the newspaper. It's good public relations for the business and just a nice thing to do. Besides, these companies are funding the education of their future employees and future executives. When they give, they are building their business community.

Allies on Television

Television stations also make public service announcements. Keep your ears tuned when watching TV. If you are not at home or do not have time to listen to the evening news, you can log on to your favorite news station's Web site. On it, they list the evening's news stories. A quick scan will tell you if any scholarships or college opportunities were announced.

Allies where you shop

The next time you go shopping, keep free money at the top of your list. Watch for posters announcing scholarships. Many retailers and food manufacturers offer scholarship programs for employees and for customers. Target Stores, McDonalds, Coca Cola, and Big Y food stores come to mind. In addition, check out the Web sites of your favorite clothing stores, grocery stores, car dealerships, fast food chains, music stores, movie theaters, and others to see if they offer scholarships to their patrons. Any place where you spend money can be a potential ally to help bankroll your dream. Pay attention! Ask questions!

Allies at the Library

The public librarian in your city or town should become your new best friend. Many libraries publish lists of scholarship and grant opportunities weekly or monthly. Oftentimes, they also publish weekly e-letters chock full of information you can use. Just get on their e-mail address list and look over what you get each week. Of course, you are looking for grants, scholarships and college- related opportunities.

Allies at Your Church or Synagogue

Don't forget church or temple. Did you know that most religious organizations offer scholarships to students in their congregations? Some offer the money through a national application process, while others offer the scholarship directly through the local church or temple. The church trustees take the money directly from the treasury of the church. If you are a member, your church can help pay your way to college, and what the church scholarship fund cannot provide may be referred to someone else who can help. Church members are a fabulous network of allies.

If you are going to take charge, it is important to realize that you have allies for your goals in many places. Your allies are there to help you financially, provide tutorial services, serve as mentors, and sometimes just cheer you on. It is essential to your success that you allow everyone who will help to pitch in and do so. You see, you are not in this alone. So pay attention!

Use this time to find out just how resourceful and resilient you are. You will surprise yourself. What you discover about yourself will be immensely helpful to you in the future. People love to support a winner. Your allies are waiting to help you.

Make a list of possible allies in your community

Name   **Location**

_____   _____

_____   _____

_____   _____

_____   _____

_____   _____

_____   _____

_____   _____

_____   _____

Tips for contacting your allies.

1. Research the names, mailing addresses, and email addresses of potential allies. Write down the name of the contact person for each organization, and be careful to spell the name correctly using the proper title.

2. Type a one-page letter for each of the individual allies. Tell him or her of your goals and why you need help. If the letter is about a scholarship opportunity, say so. Before closing the letter, thank the potential donor for his/her time and attention to your request.

3. Match envelopes with your stationary. Type all addresses and return addresses on the envelopes, or use labels.

4. If the ally suggests email correspondence, comply. Be sure to use the same proper grammatical structure and format that you would use in a letter or memo. Do not use abbreviations or "email talk". Use Standard English.

5. Avoid telephone calls on the initial contact. Follow up your letter with a phone call unless the ally discourages it. If you have to leave a message, say your name and telephone number slowly and clearly particularly if you are calling someone in another part of the country where the accent may be different from yours.

5

ORGANIZING YOUR WORKSPACE

Student

You are getting ready to do something great. You will need an organized place to work. There is something about order that makes everything easier. In order, there is room for creativity, intuition, and a relaxed sense of control over the circumstances, all of which will be needed on this adventure.

You might still wonder why you need to stop now and organize your space. You are only going to fill out a lot of forms, address envelopes, and send them off, right? Wrong. Simply finding applications and filling them out in hard copy or online will get you a college admission. That is true. But it will not place you into a college that is just right for you, your dreams, and your values.

Once you begin your college search, your home will be flooded with mail, e-mails, and phone messages, and that does not begin to include the paper that you will generate yourself, all while completing homework assignments. So your workspace must be efficient. You will need to purchase a few items.

Shopping List

1. 3 Colorful Crates or boxes
2. file folders, plain or bright colors
3. black pens
4. plain postcards
5. colored pencils
6. post its
7. white printer paper
8. stapler
9. paper clips
10 yellow highlighter
11. rolodex or small box
12. poster board, corkboard, bulletin board, or yarn

How to Use Your Supplies

First, you're going to need a place to store all of the paper, pamphlets, brochures, and business cards that you will receive. File cabinets are good, but they also keep everything out of sight and, thus, out of reach. **Colorful crates** can be very helpful because you can designate certain colors for certain items and still have everything in full view. **Three crates** should be enough. You'll also need a set of **file folders**. You may choose plain ones or bright colors. A couple of **black pens** are a must. Black ink is so much easier to read than other colors. Admissions personnel frequently make multiple copies of your correspondence and black ink copies better. Application forms or postcards requesting information should always be completed in black ink. Don't forget **two extra pens in ink of**

your favorite color for your journal and special notes.

Pick up some **post its, white printer paper** for your computer, a **stapler, paper clips,** and a **yellow highlighter**. Try to find a highlighter with a pen at the other end—it will come in handy when taking notes at a recruiting session. If you have a **Rolodex**, that's great. If not, a **small box** to hold business cards will work just as well. You can also tack business cards to a **poster board, corkboard,** or **bulletin board**, or simply string up the business cards on a **cord** to hang on the wall. Hanging boards can be helpful because they give you an immediate visual of things to do and people to meet.

You can use most of the items that you purchase for schoolwork too, so this will be money well spent. Just think, giving up the cost of just two CDs will probably pay for everything. However, if money is still a little tight, consider shopping at yard sales, tag sales, or thrift shops. Try the Goodwill Stores and the Salvation Army. These are great places to find many of these items at a fraction of the cost.

Now that the shopping is done, it's time to organize your space. Although your parents may offer input and guidance, you should organize the workspace yourself. You could set up a space in a corner of the den or family room; however, a corner of your bedroom is more ideal. A space like this will need straightening periodically. I would suggest dedicating a few minutes per week to managing your space.

Time to Organize

1. **Clear off a shelf on your bookcase for the catalogues you'll receive from colleges.**

2. **Personalize your space with posters or banners from your favorite colleges.**

Colleges love to give out posters, banners, pens, calendars, note pads, and other publicity items free. It is a good way to decorate your space, and a good way to keep your focus on the prize while cutting down the cost of office supplies.

3. **Arrange college catalogues on your bookshelf in alphabetical order.**

When you've finished browsing through brochures and other publications, put them back in their crate. When you've eliminated a particular college from your search, take the catalogue or brochure to your high school guidance counselor. Another student may be able to make good use of it. Some guidance counselors may not have time to order all of the catalogues that they would like to have, so you will also be providing a service to your school's counseling program.

4. **Check your rolodex and review your business cards.**

Discard those you won't be using. Be careful not to discard the cards of possible allies.

5. **Keep your bulletin board clear of outdated notices.**

A cluttered bulletin board contributes to chaos. Remember that it is a visual of future tasks for your project. Post notices of future events such as college fairs and recruiting sessions on your board and in your planner.

6. **Choose a quote that will keep you focused on your goal and motivated to actualize your vision.**

You may use a quotation from your favorite author or create a success statement yourself. I have created a few to jump-start the process for you. Try them on for size, then create some of your own.

- **There are no obstacles that can keep me from achieving my goal. I can see myself on the perfect college campus having extraordinary academic success, enjoying my classes, totally involved, and participating in satisfying social activities.**

- **Look out world. Here I come. I have been accepted to the best college in the world for me, and I accomplish great things while I am there. I am appreciated and enjoy my social interactions.**

- **I am destined for greatness. This is the first step on that journey.**

- Everyday, I take ordinary steps that lead to extraordinary results. I see myself in the college of my dreams learning wonderfully exciting things and surrounded by people who appreciate me.

- Everything that I do right now is laying the foundation for something awesome. The college that I seek needs me as much as I need it. I make great contributions there and make lasting friendships.

- My grand purpose is just waiting to unfold. The college that I choose is the best place for me, where my talents and gifts shine and my leadership skills are applauded.

Think about what you want to accomplish. Put it in the form of a present tense statement, and read it daily.

Words to Inspire You

1._____

_____

_____

2._____

_____

_____

3._____

_____

_____

4._____
_____
_____

5._____
_____
_____

You could create your own poster with your affirmation and hang it on the wall in the middle of the posters and banners from your favorite college. You can add artwork to your poster or other items that hold a special meaning for you. In addition, write your statement or affirmation in your daily planner and in your journal. It will serve as a reminder during the day to align your thoughts, words, and activities with the vision you have for yourself. This affirmation along with your vision statement will prove to be powerful motivators. Many successful people started their journey with affirmations. This is the first step in organizing the next and actually the most powerful space: your mind.

6

Your Skills and Interests

Student

Just as you have ordered your workspace, you must order your thoughts. When your mind and thoughts are prepared and ready to pursue a task, everything seems easier. This takes a little time, but focusing on this task now rather than later will start you on a practice that will benefit you for the rest of your life.

Why do you want to go to college in the first place? Think about this carefully. Your heartfelt reasons for pursuing this goal will sustain you when things are tough or when you are not having fun. Think about *your* reasons, not someone else's. Another person's reasons will only take you part of the way on this journey. Your reasons, even if you alter them, will carry you all the way.

What do you hope to accomplish with a college degree? If you're not absolutely sure, don't worry. This work in progress may continue for a lifetime. You can change your reasons whenever you want to change them. If you do, just be sure that you are changing your reasons because you want to. Right now, let's examine your skills and interests.

Carolyn Croom Baker

INVENTORY OF SKILLS AND INTERESTS

1. Which high school subjects bring you the most joy?

_____

_____

_____

2. What do you like to read about in your leisure time?

_____

_____

_____

3. What questions inspire your passions?

_____

_____

_____

4. What world problems would you like to solve?

_____

_____

_____

5. What societal need would you like to fill?

_____

_____

_____

6. What would make this world a better place, and how can you help?

_____

_____

_____

7. Which activities make you feel the most powerful, successful, or committed? These could be school related, extracurricular, social, civic, or spiritual.

_____

_____

_____

_____

8. What just makes your heart sing?

_____

_____

_____

_____

9. What keeps you smiling?

_____

_____

_____

_____

10. In what area are you most competent? This could be academic, social, civic, creative, or anything else that you want to consider.

_____

_____

_____

These questions help you know yourself better. If you answer honestly, they provide valuable clues to your life's mission or at least to what you should try first. Remember, nothing is carved in granite. You can change your mind. As long as you are being true to yourself and progressing forward, you can't lose. Some of the most successful people on the planet have had lots of different educational experiences, changed college majors, and changed careers. Every new experience leads to the next success.

While we're in the contemplative mode, let's look at some practical steps to learning more about you. If you are not expressing yourself in all of the areas that you listed above, explore some of your interests through your high school's extracurricular offerings. If working with art, singing in the shower, or perhaps imitating odd human or animal voices puts a permanent smile on your face, then take the opportunity to try art classes at your school, a theater group, or the glee club. You might find that one of these things is more than a passing interest.

Don't laugh at the animal voice suggestion. There was a young woman on a TV talk show who clucked like a chicken. Clucking on national television changed her life. She clucked and laughed all the way to the bank. So don't discount any talent.

While you are still in high school and the stakes are not too high, take the time to explore these ten questions and review your answers periodically. Make adjustments, changes, or corrections whenever you feel the need to do so.

SKILLS AND INTERESTS INVENTORY: PART 2

List specific activities when you used your skills or explored your interests

Skill	Activity
_____	_____
_____	_____
_____	_____
_____	_____
_____	_____

Interest	Activity
_____	_____
_____	_____
_____	_____
_____	_____
_____	_____

List five new ways to use your skills and explore your interests

Skills and Interests	Activities
_____	_____
_____	_____
_____	_____
_____	_____
_____	_____

Parents

Some parents are very generous with their children and teach their children to trust their own instincts. Others feel that they know best and try to prescribe their child's future, all in the name of love. Some parents try to determine their child's college and major, all too often without regard for their child's thoughts or passions. When this happens, the process is a lot more arduous than it needs to be and the child, oftentimes as an adult, will still have to come back to square one and discover his or her true path.

I cannot emphasize enough the importance of honoring your child's personal vision. Over the years, I have seen countless young lives sidetracked and hijacked by someone else's unfulfilled dreams. I know of a young man who went to college, majored in microbiology, graduated, and continued that field of study in graduate school. His true love was music. That is where he works today but only after years of stress, disappointment, and personal frustration. Another young woman studied political science in college and then went on to law school. She graduated from law school, studied for and passed the bar exam, and then practiced law for a number of years. Her heart, however, was in teaching. She didn't want to disappoint her parents, so she continued working in a law firm. After many sleepless nights, she finally left law to teach high school history. She is happy now that she's following her dream and not her father's.

We all know numerous stories like this. One of us might even have lived through one of them. We have seen dramatic examples on TV talk shows. There was the story of the lawyer who gave up his federal position to bake cakes. He looked very happy on national television surrounded by the hundreds of cakes he had baked. He said that he knew that baking was a calling for him. Many of the titles on the list of best selling how-to books lead back to this moment in time when a few well-guided hours of introspection could have made all the difference.

I discovered a wonderful book by Mark Albion, *Making a Life, Making a Living: Reclaiming Your Purpose and Passion in Business and In Life*. In it he talks about the importance of honoring your own passions and intentions for your life. He discusses a 20-year study of 1500 business school graduates. The study divided the 1500 graduates into two categories: (A) those who chose careers based on expected financial reward and (B) those who followed their true interests or passions. At final count, 83 percent (1,245 graduates) chose category A, and only 17 percent (255 graduates) chose category B. After 20 years, the researcher discovered 101 millionaires in the group of 1500 graduates. There was one millionaire in category A and 100 millionaires in category B. According to this study, wealth really is a by-product of following one's passions and true interests.

This is a fertile time for parent and child communication, when your child can have your uninterrupted attention for a truly valuable discussion. Respect, cherish, and honor this time. Give it its own place on your planner. Look at all of the activities of the week and determine the best hour to work on this. Just one hour per week can provide an invaluable life lesson. Then, compare planners and set the time. Let nothing interfere with this appointment.

Parents and students have an important role to play in this process. Make sure to give each role its due respect. In a few short years or maybe even next year, you will not have this option. Your child will have obligations that will not involve you. Parents can support students best by being there as an advocate and listener.

Truth telling exercises are therapeutic for both parents and students. It may give your child more insight to hear some of your stories about what worked for you and what did not. Your stories may also provide a platform from which your child can explore answers to his or her questions.

7

Practical Acts.....Course Scheduling

Parents and Student

According to the College Board, students who pursue the most rigorous plan of study in high school have the greatest chance for success in college. University and college admissions officers also agree that the courses taken in high school are the most valid indicators of future success at the college level. There are very few exceptions to that rule.

Most high schools allow students to choose courses in the late winter or early spring for the following school year. This is an ideal time to talk about which courses will lead to the final goal, and which courses will help to position you for admission to the right college. Many high schools also allow students to select courses for the second semester a month or two before the semester begins. So, there may be two opportunities to review your plan of study and to make sure that together you choose the right ones. Rigor is the key word.

Even students in the eighth grade have the opportunity to choose courses for high school. High school guidance counselors meet with eighth graders at various points in the year to assist them in the transition to high school. Although the middle school counselor usually plans the high school course of study, the high school counselor contributes to that process.

Student

The National Association of College Admissions Counselors estimates that there will be two million students entering college in the fall. Of course, more will apply. Now granted, not all of those applicants have the same goals that you have. After all, you want more from your education than a degree and a college transcript worthy of admission to a good graduate school. You want a space where you can learn more about you, where you will discover a way to bring your special message, your gifts and talents to the world.

You need a place that will also allow you to grow and expand while you lead and serve. Yes, you are a different case, but you will still be competing for a prized spot in the freshman class with all of the other college applicants in this country. In addition, you will compete with thousands of foreign nationals who apply to college in the United States every year. Foreign students generally understand and practice rigor from an early age and speak multiple languages. Many colleges actively recruit foreign nationals because they have less need for financial aid or scholarships. In other words, it is a very profitable thing for the colleges to do.

Parents and Student

This is what college admissions officers expect to see as a minimum course of high school study:

English: four years

Mathematics: three years

Science: three years, including a year of a laboratory science, one year of a life science, and one physical science.

Social Studies: three years, including world history, some study of United States Government, and some United States History.

Foreign language: one or two years

The Arts: advisable and frequently required

Physical Education: credits set by the state

Electives: courses that you choose according to personal interest

Most school districts will require the aforementioned courses for graduation from their schools. So, students will have to take these subjects. Aim for more than the minimum. Aim for the highest level or most advanced courses in these subjects.

Some schools separate students according to ability levels. This is called homogeneous or ability grouping. In other words, students of similar ability are grouped together in all academic courses. Other schools allow students to take courses according to goals and personal preference. This is called heterogeneous grouping. In a heterogeneous grouping, classes are filled with students from a variety of academic levels—from high to low. If your school groups students homogeneously, your course of study will be prescribed by your results on certain standardized tests and, frequently, teacher recommendations. Usually in schools like this, you take certain tests that rate your competence in reading, vocabulary, writing, mathematics, and reasoning. Test results are usually available a month or two after the test date. Teachers, administrators, and guidance counselors then use your scores to group you for class assignments. Once you are grouped, your test scores will determine the level of academic challenge that you will be allowed to pursue in the required academic areas.

Here is what I suggest:

English

Ask for and pursue the most difficult English courses your school offers each year. Of all the required courses, in my view, English is the most essential for future academic success as well as future success in character-building activities. In English classes, you develop reading comprehension, analytical ability, writing skills, expanded vocabulary, and public speaking skills. You learn about literature from a variety of sources and develop a facility for both oral and written expression.

English classes at all levels strive to meet certain objectives that are driven by the State Department of Education's performance standards. The lower level classes demand less writing and literary analysis than the upper level classes. What does this all mean for you? Students in a lower level class learn fewer new vocabulary words and read less complex material. Opportunities for public speaking are there, but generally, the more sophisticated forms of self-expression will not be the focus. That said, it is important to remember that sometimes, ability grouping can serve a good purpose. A slower paced class may be most appropriate for students who have some academic deficiencies or who find certain subjects more difficult than others. That student might pursue rigor in another area.

All students should attempt to take more than the minimum requirement for graduation from high school. Try an extra writing, poetry, or literature course. Students who qualify should take the senior year advanced placement (AP) English course. What about a debate course or public speaking course if your school offers that? Your guidance counselor can discuss which English courses fulfill the graduation requirement and which ones can serve as electives.

Mathematics

Since this subject area can be a little tricky, it is important to start focusing on mathematics early in the middle school. Make sure that you take more than the minimum mathematics requirements for graduation. Mathematics, unlike English, is sequential. Success in the current class depends on skills learned in the previous class. So, once you are on a particular track, it's hard to change directions. The college preparatory sequence is as follows:

Algebra I

Geometry

Algebra II

Pre- Calculus

Calculus

Advanced placement (AP) mathematics

More advanced mathematics

Many high schools offer variations on this sequence. Some schools offer a pre-algebra course before the algebra I course. Some offer algebra II before geometry. Others offer a calculus course without a pre-calculus course. Carefully read the course selection descriptions before you agree to a certain program of study.

Middle school course work plays a major role in the process. In many school districts, talented mathematics students are able to start the college preparatory mathematics sequence in the seventh grade: they take algebra I, followed by geometry in the eighth grade. By the time that student reaches ninth grade, he or she is ready for algebra II. A sequence like this allows a student to pursue three additional years of advanced study in mathematics, thus strengthening the high school transcript even more. Of course, students who are on this particular track are excellent math students and are willing to work hard. Although it is important to accept a challenge, students should not insist on taking courses for which they are not prepared.

Students who are not advanced math students should choose from a number of other options. They might take pre-algebra in the 7th grade, followed by algebra I in the 8th grade, leading to geometry in the 9th grade. This sort of sequence prepares students for algebra II in the 10th grade and leaves two additional years for more advanced study in mathematics.

If the focus of the student's middle school mathematics program is to build a strong foundation for high school study, he or she may not be allowed to take algebra I until 9th grade. Algebra I will be followed by geometry in the sophomore year and algebra II in the junior year, leaving the senior year for more advanced study in mathematics. As you can see, the sequence remains the same. The timing for course work may vary.

In high school, there are a myriad other math courses from which to choose. For example, there may be a number of business math courses. There are also integrated math courses, where you study a blend of algebra and geometry for three years. These courses are generally not as rigorous and counselors schedule them for the student who might need a little more support in math. For students who thrive on challenge, take the college preparatory sequence listed on the previous page.

If you know that you can handle more challenging work than you're being offered, tell your guidance counselor that you want to take more courses that are difficult. It is essential, however, that you let reason be your guide. If you have deficits in your math background, give the school the opportunity to correct those deficits before moving forward. Get tutorial services to supplement what you are learning in school. If tutorial fees cost too much, look for volunteers such as peer tutors, college students, neighbors, or teachers. Some retired teachers also volunteer to tutor students. **Teachers in your child's school may volunteer to help hard working students after school, before school, or during lunch.**

Athletes who hope to play a sport in college should make sure to take the minimum of algebra I, geometry, and algebra II before graduating from high school. The NCAA requires these courses for participation in the athletic programs of many colleges.

Carolyn Croom Baker

The transcript for college admissions begins at grade nine. This is the year to show ambition and motivation to study harder. The more math courses a student takes, the more confident he or she will feel when completing college admissions tests. I told you earlier about how the SAT had changed. At one point, arithmetic, algebra I, geometry, and some algebra II questions were the only areas of math to consider when preparing for the college admissions tests. The mathematics sections of the SAT and ACT are more difficult now, and students will face more algebra II questions.

So what does all this mean for parents and students when planning a course of study? Parents can ensure that their child's course of study is correct and continues in a forward motion. Arrange a meeting with the guidance counselor at the beginning, middle, and end of the school year. Many parents will not call and ask for such a meeting. Some may work out of town or be otherwise committed. Some just will not think to make the call. So, you will certainly be able to get an appointment. You and Tricia's mom, that is. The mid-year meeting is particularly important because many high schools change course schedules again in January. Parents need to be there to advocate for the rigor of their child's schedule.

So, what happens if for some reason a student simply can't handle the rigor of a college preparatory mathematics sequence? Don't worry. Although many colleges, particularly selective colleges and state universities require math through at least algebra II, many colleges will be happy to accept students without that much math. Many colleges focus on the whole student. Standardized test scores or grades in one subject such as mathematics will not prevent students from attending a good college. Community colleges take a liberal attitude toward mathematics requirements for admission, as do some private colleges. Just be aware that less math will affect the college admissions test score, the SAT, or the ACT.

The most important thing to remember is that parents must encourage students to take the most difficult courses that they can manage. Challenging high school courses prepare students for more difficult college level work. In addition, colleges have course requirements that entering students must fulfill. College freshmen are frequently given placement tests upon entry. Some colleges use the SAT or ACT scores for placement purposes. If the student's mathematics or English achievement is not up to the college's standard, the student may be required to take remedial courses.

Remedial courses are designed to make up for deficiencies that were not corrected at the high school level. Although remedial courses can be helpful, students take them without academic credit, yet the cost of the course is the same as the cost of a full credit course. If remedial courses are included in the freshman academic schedule, then something else is not, and that means that parents will be paying for something that will not count toward graduation from college. Required courses will be delayed until all remedial requirements are met.

Science

College admissions officers expect to see at least three credits of science. Colleges expect, and most high schools require, one course in a life science such as biology, and one course in a physical science such as chemistry or physics. Most high schools have other options. Usually, biology is the first course followed by chemistry and then physics. Mathematics competency directs the level of the science courses. Some mathematics competency is required for success in physics.

Students should take the most demanding science courses that they can handle. It is not only of benefit to the students; it is of benefit to the academic standing of this country. Many technical and science–oriented jobs are now outsourced to certain foreign countries because many foreign students are more prepared to be academically competitive in today's market. Granted, that might not be the only reason for the outsourcing business practice, but it certainly is a major one. Students of character and leadership have an even greater responsibility to be academically prepared to be in this nation's top positions.

High school academic initiative implies future college initiative and future drive to excel. Once you meet the high school graduation requirements, take additional science courses. Aim to complete the graduation requirements at the highest level that the high school offers, and then continue with even more advanced courses. A transcript that includes additional coursework beyond what is expected or required demonstrates academic initiative, a quality that college admissions officers will appreciate.

For example, if your school offers biology, college prep biology, and honors biology, and you have a choice, choose the most challenging of the three. Do the same for the other science courses. Advanced Placement (AP) courses are taken following the successful completion of the regular curriculum. If you take honors science classes in grades 9, 10, and 11, you will be eligible to take AP science courses in grade 12. Ambitious science students may choose to take an AP course earlier or even multiple ones. All students who can should try to conclude their high school science curriculum with Advance Placement courses.

You can expect high schools to offer several AP courses in science, usually AP biology, AP chemistry, and AP physics. High schools that emphasize the sciences offer an even wider variety of AP courses. Students have the opportunity to choose according to their area of interest. If there is any chance at all that you will pursue a college major in the sciences, medicine, technology, or engineering, advanced science and mathematics courses will be crucial.

Science courses provide an excellent opportunity to strengthen analytical skills and higher order critical thinking. Both are competencies that will be needed in college.

History

Students who value character development and who want to take a leadership role in the future will need to understand the rudiments of American history. Most schools require a 9th grade course in American and local government. Everyone, especially future leaders, should understand how government works, what works best, and what may need to be changed. It is highly unlikely that leaders will bring about responsible change without a comprehensive understanding of how America was formed and the structure of our government.

In the 10th grade, students begin a study of U. S. history. This course covers history from the first arrivals of Europeans on American shores to the U. S. Civil War. In this course, students learn how the country was founded, what obstacles were overcome, and which ones were not. Students study a second program of U. S. history in the junior year, which covers American history from the Civil War through the Civil Rights movement of the 1960s, or a bit later. At some point during the high school career, students will also study world history, usually an overview of world cultures.

The names and sequence of the various American history, world history, and American government courses may vary from state to state and among school districts within the states. Even the structure of the courses may be different. Some examine themes within a historical context. Others look at historical events in chronological order. Whatever the case, students must take some form of U. S. government, U. S. history, and world history. Again, our focus is rigor. Insist on taking the most rigorous courses you can handle. Frequently, curriculum specialists assign history courses according to academic proficiency. Students who score well on the standardized tests that we mentioned earlier will be encouraged to take more advanced history courses, while others will pursue less challenging courses. Academic challenge is essential for your success.

Parents and students must walk a fine line between academic challenge and appropriate placement. To build academic muscle, rigor is essential. Too much, however, can break the spirit. Parents and students need to sit down together and be honest with each other. How much work can the student really handle? Remember that high school is a time for intellectual preparation for college. College courses are not ability grouped. You sign up for a history class, and you take what you get. High school is the time, while the risk is low, to build on your skills and abilities so that you are ready to be competitive. Absolutely nothing builds a student's confidence faster than feeling competent and knowing he or she can actively participate in a discussion with the best that the school has and be on par with everyone else.

Carolyn Croom Baker

Plan to take at least one extra history class. High school departments of history, like all of the others, offer other courses beyond the required ones. Advanced history courses demand a lot of writing and therefore strengthen writing skills. Advanced students should absolutely think about taking an AP history course. It could be AP U. S. history, AP government, psychology, or some other course that interests you. Advanced Placement courses give you an edge over other students. They show the college admissions officers that you are willing to take on a challenge. It also gives you college credits if you score well on the AP exam. That means you will get college credits for free or for just the cost of the Advanced Placement exam.

History courses also help you to understand the culture in which you live. You learn about the genesis of American values, how Americans think, and why Americans happen to think that way. You also develop a clearer understanding of politics and how your local government works or at least how it should work. As future leaders, political understanding will be invaluable to you.

Foreign Language

Students of conscience and character should take every opportunity to prepare for their place in a global society. Learning a new language is a good first start. President Richard Levin in his fall address to Yale University's 2006 freshmen class urged the native English-speaking students to master a foreign language and to make every effort to spend time abroad working or studying. Twenty-first century challenges will demand a multinational collaborative effort. Foreign language mastery can be the foundation for understanding other cultures, which leads to greater cooperation on issues that matter to us all.

Foreign language proficiency is a marketable skill. To be able to put that skill on a resume is a great thing and can mean more money in your pocket later on. The communications industry and air travel have made our planet seem smaller and smaller. Many companies today think nothing of relocating employees abroad or having employees travel to far flung areas of the globe to market a new product.

Even if you don't plan to work for a multi-national corporation, you can never predict where work will lead. For students who plan to take a leadership role in society, travel will more than likely be a part of your life whether for a conference, a business deal, a presentation, or just for vacation. I cannot emphasize enough the value of taking foreign language courses. Some school districts require a foreign language to graduate from high school. Others do not.

The United States is also still receiving large numbers of internationals for residency. Colleges and universities are no exception. Admissions offices in many colleges invest a lot of money to recruit foreign students because international students don't need as much financial help. Those students are expected to be able to carry their own weight. You will probably interact with a number of international students on campus and may have a foreign-born roommate. Most international students come to this country able to speak several languages. International students are now competitors with you for the same jobs upon graduation from college. They will be able to read, write, and speak in their own language, in English, and in one or two other languages. Many international students return home after college to lead in the progress of their own country. Many stay right here. You definitely want to be in the front of the pack, right there with Tricia. That is where leaders are supposed to be.

Foreign Language study can and should start no later than middle school. Some students start even earlier. Students learn new languages very easily when they are young. The other benefit is improved English vocabulary, leading to improved college admissions test scores. You might wonder how the study of another language can improve scores on the SAT or ACT. Our language has Latin, French, and some German roots. The study of Latin or any of the romance languages, including French, Spanish, or Italian will help you understand the meaning of English words. Students who have studied French, for example, may see a word on the SAT or ACT that they do not know and be able to deduce the meaning, because they studied Latin and, therefore, know the root meaning of the word. The same is true for students who study German, other European, or classical languages.

Students who start foreign language study in middle school may be able to get high school credit for the courses they complete. The more credits students can get early on, the less they will have to pay for later. Although most colleges expect to see at least two years of a foreign language, students should take more. So, let's say that a student starts in middle school and takes French I or maybe even takes French I and French II. That student will be eligible to take French III in the first year of high school.

You might wonder why this student should have to take French III in the ninth grade when most colleges only require two years of a foreign language for admission. First, courses taken in middle school will not show up on the high school transcript. The high school will know that the student studied French for two years before coming to high school, the student will know, and the school counselor will know, but there will be no way for the college to know that the student studied a foreign language unless it's taken in high school. Second, you want to be competitive. I know I have said that a lot and I will continue to emphasize it. It is essential that you stand out above the crowd. Leaders always do.

Just a comment or two about leadership: Leaders in schools, businesses, organizations, civic groups, or government are rarely the most brilliant, the most talented, or even the hardest working. They are people who are confident enough to share the skills they have, and they have the ability to motivate others to share their own skills. Leaders are usually multitalented. They have a sense of curiosity and a willingness to try new things. They harness all of their skills to get a job done, and they know how to get others to do the same. You may not be able to speak French like a native, but if you try to learn a new language, that impresses college admissions officers, particularly if you take on the truly unfamiliar. For example, a student who takes the familiar Spanish or French and adds a year or two of Chinese or Japanese study is sure to appear unique in a sea of applicants.

So, back to the sequence. After completing the foreign language course in the 9th grade, students should take as many more years of that same language as possible. Some students may be tempted to take several languages but only the first and maybe second year of each. Therefore, when they graduate, they will have four or even five years of foreign language study, but they may only have two or three years of two different languages. This is not a good strategy. Colleges want students who consistently attempt increasingly difficult work. Remember, you will need to compete with very advanced students who may have four years of one language and six years of another.

Students who experience competency in the study of a foreign language should take the most advanced courses available. Take an AP foreign language course if your school offers it. Take two if you can handle it. Students are generally eligible for an AP foreign language course after completing five or more years of study of the same language. Some schools offer both AP literature courses and AP language use courses. A good score on the AP exam will not only look great on the transcript and demonstrate ambition; it may provide college credit. **You may not need to take a foreign language in college just because you were able to perform so well in high school.** You will advance in a very important life skill: the ability to communicate in another language.

If for some reason foreign language study is extremely difficult for you, don't force it. There are plenty of great colleges that don't require a foreign language to be admitted, neither do they require foreign language study at their school.

Electives

Some students naturally want an academic challenge and will always ask for the most rigorous courses the high school has to offer. Such students were like that even in elementary school. Others will need to be convinced that challenge and rigor are the two best routes to success. For parents who are looking to educate with character in mind, there are additional considerations when mapping out a course of study. Make sure there is room in the schedule for elective courses that speak to leadership, civic responsibility, and personal evolvement.

Your choice of electives tells the college a lot about you; therefore, it is important to give electives serious thought. Many students look at electives as just fluff courses. This is definitely not the case. Look at your natural talents. Perhaps there is a subject you would like to explore without stress or risk. This is the time. Electives can also be used to strengthen abilities in academic areas. For example, suppose you have an interest in science and hope to become a scientist or health care provider. Take an extra science course or two. There is usually enough room in the high school course of study to take a good number of elective courses in a variety of subjects.

The beauty of taking electives is that students are likely to discover new talents, interests, or even passions that were previously unknown. How many great actors discovered their talent in a high school drama course? Journalism classes may help some students uncover a talent for writing.

Colleges want to see that you are well rounded, but not unfocused. If, for example, you want a pre-med major in college, and you have an interest in art, focus some of the elective courses in art. It demonstrates that you have other interests and are willing to invest the time to develop them.

Elective courses can also be coordinated with extracurricular activities. For example, if you take a number of music classes and you are also in extracurricular music activities, that is a demonstration of consistency and commitment. You are also sharing your talent with the school community, which will build your confidence and make the school community richer. Colleges might seek you out with the hope that you'll contribute to the musical life of their campus. If you are a truly gifted musician, you might also be eligible for scholarships.

Make sure that you take a few electives every year. Some students are tempted to take all their academic subjects first and save electives for the senior year. Avoid this temptation. This may not be welcome advice for some seniors who were hoping to cruise through their senior year. Don't cruise! Drive! Run! Keep the same pace in senior year as in earlier years. It is true that your transcript may not show senior grades, but senior courses will be highlighted and report cards will be attached. You don't want prospective colleges to see a lazy senior.

In schools where they still **rank students**, it is tempting to avoid electives because they frequently carry less weight than academic subjects carry and can negatively affect the **Grade Point Average (GPA)**. Your GPA is that magic number all admissions officers want to see. In schools where they rank students and weight the courses, this is an important issue. In reality, the effect of electives on the GPA is minimal. If you attend one of the enlightened high schools where students are not ranked, you do not have to worry about receiving a lower rank due to elective courses. Colleges will be able to see that you are an interesting person with a curious intellect and a desire to explore new things. You will have the opportunity to try new skills and perhaps discover, or uncover a talent that you didn't know you had.

Electives provide the opportunity to experiment with learning. Great chefs can be discovered in a culinary arts class and opera singers in a music class. One of my former students, who is now a celebrated opera singer, discovered her musical talent in high school just by trying a new music class. She was fortunate to have the support of her parents while she experimented with learning something new. Her life today is rich and full of passion for her work, and she's an inspiration for many aspiring musicians. What if she had never tried?

8

EXTRACURRICULAR ACTIVITIES

Student

Take an active role in your school and community. It helps you to develop life skills, talents, confidence, and leadership skills. Being involved in school activities also teaches you how to work collaboratively with your peers and adults, a necessary skill for future success. Research shows that students who are actively engaged in school and community activities achieve higher grades and are better time managers. That benefit alone is enough reason to get involved. However, the lasting benefits have even greater value.

Extracurricular activities include sports, clubs, and civic organizations within the school, as well as the arts. In fact, the College Board researched the correlation between arts study and SAT scores and found that **students who pursue courses in music and the visual arts frequently score higher on college entrance exams than students who do not**. That's a benefit. Through theater and music programs, students learn to be less self-conscious, and to feel comfortable on the larger stage. The larger stage is just the place a leader will be many times in the future.

The visual arts will allow you to reach inside of yourself for that creative spark. Visual arts study provides a place where students can express their creativity freely and have it nourished. We all know the value of team sports. We have heard the coaches talk about the discipline, cooperative spirit, and teamwork that sports teach. Through sports, students can learn to think on behalf of the group and depart from the individualistic approach that dominated so much of their thinking in their younger years.

Did you know that students who study dance develop better non-verbal reasoning skills? Non-verbal reasoning skills are essential in fields like engineering, science, architecture, and other fields that require assessing visual information. Dance is a good program for lifetime fitness, poise, and grace. Besides, upon entering a room, a dancer understands how to command the space. Presence is an invaluable quality.

The College Board reports that students who have coursework in music score 60 points higher on the verbal portion of the SAT and 40 points higher on the mathematics section than their non-artistic peers. Music study increases spatial/temporal-reasoning skills that are important in studying mathematics. Music study also increases a student's quality of writing. See the College Board Web site for more information. Visual arts students can improve reading skills, and drama students develop social skills, problem solving skills, and self-confidence.

Get involved in extracurricular activities as early in your high school career as possible. Colleges like to see longevity and continuity. A student who starts playing in the school band in the ninth grade and continues into senior year is much more attractive and interesting than the student who played in the band one year, sang in the choir one year, and played football another year. Students who jump from one activity to another show a lack of commitment and focus. College admission officers make note of that. They are definitely not impressed by a sudden flurry of extracurricular activity in the senior year. **The words to remember here are longevity and continuity.**

Of course, if you haven't participated in any extracurricular activities and you have good reasons, this can be explained in the college essay. If you have no reason, get involved in a service project. Service projects satisfy a need and allow you to accomplish something of value in a short time. The point is to take action whenever you can or whenever you learn the lesson. It is never too late to get on the right track. Simply take responsibility for poor decisions and move on. **Get involved and make a contribution.**

Parents

You play a major role in the choice of extracurricular activities. As a professional counselor, I understand the need that parents have to keep their offspring safe from stress by allowing students to cling to the familiar. But, guess what? It's hard to develop your best self while confined to your comfort zone. Experimenting with new venues for self-expression teaches great lessons and uncovers new talents. Most schools have dozens of clubs, sports, organizations, and arts groups through which students can safely experiment with new talents. The risk-taking may seem great, but it is really minimal compared to future risks; and colleges will be glad to see that they tried.

As school budgets shrink under the weight of so many demands, it is also essential that parents lobby school district administrators to maintain arts curricula and good arts instruction.

Student

If you find no organizations in your school or community appealing, create one. You can create service projects, arts projects, or civic awareness projects to name a few. There are always people in the community who need help. A young man in my neighborhood started a volunteer lawn service for seniors. He convinced several of his fellow classmates to join with him on this venture. Now, my ninety-year-old neighbors do not have to worry about raking their own leaves or cleaning their gutters. A group of about eight high school students shows up every fall to rake and bag all of the leaves, clean the gutters, and put down mulch.

The students have a number of clients in this neighborhood who depend on their services. In return, the senior clients give the students cookies, brownies, and hot chocolate. The students get a warm feeling knowing they have provided a needed service to someone. One client gives each student a handmade potholder and a hug as her thank you. That gift puts a real smile on the students' faces, especially the boys.

Other students have started tutorial programs, reading programs, and sports programs for younger children who benefit from the attention. I know of a male quartet in one high school that donates singing time in a nursing home. Singing is their service. Imagine the smiles on the residents' faces when these good-looking, smiling, young men come in to sing. The boys have learned many of the songs from the 1940s, and the seniors love it. The young men's singing sends groups of previously inactive seniors to the dance floor. These young men bring joy and make a lot of lonely people happy.

Students who have political interests should get involved in student government, run for office, or help run a local politician's campaign. Student government organizations always plan several service projects throughout the school year. This creates opportunities for school and community service. Politicians can always use youthful energy and an extra pair of hands and feet during their political campaigns. You don't think the gubernatorial, mayoral, or congressional candidates pass out all those leaflets and conduct all those phone surveys themselves, do you? Students who decide to jump in and help will be welcome.

Part-time work is also a valued extracurricular activity. Some students cannot join clubs or get involved in sports because they must work to contribute to the family income. Don't worry. Work counts too. College admissions personnel are interested in your work experiences. Students who hold the same job for several years also show commitment, responsibility, and maturity. Babysitting for your Aunt Sarah may not count as much, but it does demonstrate some responsibility. Creating your own job is even better.

How do you create your own job? You could use your musical talents to provide entertainment for a fee in your town, and if you are a visual artist, you could sell your work. I worked with a young teen who started a landscaping business. He saved his allowance and all of his money from another part time job at the local bank. The bank, then, was receptive when he explained his business idea. He found a co-signer and borrowed $5,000 so he could purchase lawn equipment. He printed flyers and business cards and walked all over town passing them out. Remember the story of the seniors with the leaves and gutters? Well, he capitalized on that. He was hired by local businesses that needed a general clean up of their job site. He picked up the trash, mowed the grass, trimmed the hedges, pulled weeds, planted flowers, and well, you can just imagine how many other services this student could do. By senior year, he had a thriving business and was able to hire several of his classmates. That kind of initiative adds value to a resume, not to mention hefty savings.

You may be surprised to know that there are numerous scholarships for participation in extracurricular activities. I'll bet you thought that all scholarships were based on some lofty academic accomplishment. Not so. There are scholarships for golfers, bowlers, and athletes. There are scholarships for students who work on the school newspaper and perform in the school play. Take advantage of these activities. You are in for wonderful surprises on this journey.

9

THE RIGHT FIT

Student

Some lucky college is going to have the pleasure of your company for the next four years. You laid the foundation. College admissions publications market the benefits of their institutions and tell you how lucky you would be to go there. They will tell you about the student–teacher ratio, the facilities, the number of professors with terminal degrees (that's Ph.D., not end of life), their competitive status, areas of study, dormitories, and on–campus activities; but the most important question is what are you looking for in a college?

Every student who finds the right college campus finds a place to thrive, grow, and develop new talents and skills. But luck goes both ways. You know that you are a wonderful, talented, highly motivated young adult. The college will be lucky to attract you also.

Looking inside first often sheds light on the outside. It is time for a little introspection. Let's take a look at some of the questions that were suggested in the first chapter. Use your favorite color pencil. Don't censor your answers. Just let them flow freely. For this exercise, there is no right or wrong answer, only your truth as you see it. You may wonder what some of these questions have to do with getting into college. Just play along. You will see. By the way, only you can answer these questions!

WHAT DO YOU NEED IN A COLLEGE?

The first eight questions focus on the kind of physical environment you're looking for in a college.

1. What kind of personal environment do you need?

There is a campus to fill every need. It is important for you to know where you thrive best. I have heard students say that it doesn't make a difference where the school is as long as they like it. It is true that your environment may not matter while you have family support to make you feel nurtured and a part of things. When you are away from all that is familiar to you, you may need an environment that resonates more closely with your being. When parents, loved ones, pets, and familiar surroundings are absent, what will nurture your spirit, comfort you, and make you feel like you belong?

_____

_____

_____

_____

2. How close to home do you need to be?

People choose distance for different reasons, and their decision to stay near or go far is not an indictment. It's emancipation. For families who enjoy having everyone close to the hearth, a local college or state university may be the right answer. Some students thrive, feel more confident, take more of a leadership role, and develop many more of their natural talents when they are close to home and have the loving support of family. Some students need to visit home each weekend, if only to stop in for breakfast and a hug. That hug gives them the courage to take risks, stand up, and stand out.

Other students feel stifled close to home. Old friends and too many family members can stand between them and the person they wish they could be. Sometimes young people need distance and to be surrounded by strangers before they have the courage to risk showcasing new talents, exploring leadership potential, or exploring the world. What do you need?

_____

_____

_____

3. Do you prefer a country setting, a city setting, or a combination of the two?

Not sure? Ask yourself this: Are you energized by the sounds of rushing cars, buses, and teeming masses of humanity; bright lights, people out walking at midnight, a feeling of constant activity, a truly vibrant community? On the other hand, do you need a more serene setting, to be near trees, animals, rivers, oceans, or mountains, or at least know that you have access to them? What environment resonates for you?

_____

_____

If you choose a country setting, how close to a city do you need to be? Is there easy access to the city? Some colleges provide regular transportation to the nearest city or town, particularly on weekends. Some colleges encourage student participation in city activities, service projects, and cultural events. Others do not and expect students to access those things on their own. If accessing live theater, concerts, church, lectures, people and events off campus is important to you, make sure that the college that you choose makes that possible. Some don't.

4. What activities make you smile?

These are activities that bring a smile to your face at the very thought of doing them. Even if you never do them, just the thought of doing them makes you happy. Make the list as long as you like, but be sure to write down the first things that come to mind. You can do a mental sorting later.

_____

_____

_____

_____

_____

5. Why do you like thinking about these activities?

This will help you to get a better picture of what you value and what is important to you. Don't stop to think about whether or not what you write makes sense, sounds right, or is appropriate. At this point, we are only interested in your truth.

_____

_____

_____

_____

6. What activities do you simply feel compelled to do?

You do these activities without thinking. You just know that you have to do them. We all know people who doodle. They doodle without thinking. Artists do it. Writers do it even when they do not know that they are writers. There are just some things that each one of us needs to do. Some people need to work in a garden every day. They just don't feel right until they do that. Dancers must dance, and musicians must make music. Whether they choose those fields as a profession or not is irrelevant. What do you just have to do? You will look for this activity on the campuses you visit.

_____

_____

_____

7. Do you want to attend a college or a university?

What's the difference, you might ask? A college is a single school designed for study in a broad area. There are colleges of liberal arts that include study in languages; physical, life, and social sciences; English; mathematics; and the humanities.

There are colleges of pharmacy, architecture, engineering, law, medicine, dentistry, and a variety of other areas of study that may be the focus. There are colleges of fine arts for the study of visual art, music, dance, and theater. Within each of these broad areas, there are more specific areas for specialization.

Colleges may stand alone as autonomous institutions or be a part of a university. University is derived from the word universe. The universe encompasses the whole. There are planets within solar systems and systems within the universe, but none is diminished by the presence of the other. In a university, there are several colleges, each with their own focus but each contributes to the richness of the university as a whole. Universities offer opportunities to interface with students of varied disciplines.

_____

8. What size college? Not sure? Read on.

Colleges with fewer than 5,000 students are considered small. Small has nothing to do with quality of education. I have talked to students who feel that a good school is a big school. **They equate large size with quality. That is a myth. Quality comes in all sizes and so does mediocrity.** Think about your personal needs. Make decisions based upon what size school will make you feel comfortable and help you thrive.

Small schools have a number of pluses. Classes are generally smaller, there are fewer large group lectures and more small group discussions, and students have opportunity to work with professors on a more personal level. In fact, small colleges generally encourage professors to interact with students, to meet with them regularly. There are opportunities for special projects, individual conferences, and sometimes a quiet lunch to discuss an idea. Although professors on small campuses are also encouraged to write and publish, there is much more focus on teaching and getting to know their students. **Students who know that they learn best when they have the opportunity to talk with the professor and ask questions, to meet in small study groups, and to have classes in small seminar rooms may want to consider a smaller college.**

A small college also provides more opportunities for the less assertive student to participate in campus life. Competition for choral groups, theatre troupes, and other performance groups may be less intense. Administrators are more aware of students' interests and can recommend certain students for programs, internships, and travel opportunities. At a small college, good internships are generally easier to get because there are fewer students competing. I talked to a senior student at Rollins College, a small liberal arts college in Winter Park, Florida, who had completed four internships, including three abroad. She said the internships helped her decide on a career field and made her more competitive for graduate school. She also said that being in a small school helped her develop her self-confidence and leadership skills and uncover talents that she had not known.

Connecticut College, a small selective liberal arts college, encourages students to develop service projects locally, nationally, and internationally. It is true that large colleges provide similar opportunities. It is just that on smaller campuses, it is so much easier for less assertive students to access programs. It is also easier for such students to be seen by others and thus included in special programs and activities.

Medium sized colleges have between 5,000 and 15,000 students. Now 15,000 may sound like a real mass of humanity, but frequently populations of this size are on university campuses and students are spread out among several colleges. The student body may include commuters and residential students, young traditional-age students, adults, and senior citizens. Generally, older students take their classes in the evening and quickly leave campus when classes are over. These commuter students generally have full-time jobs to report to the next day and families. You won't run into the senior citizens in the student center or at the campus movie. However, you might see them in the gym. The Baby Boomers are creating a completely new group of college attendees, and they want to stay in shape.

Medium sized campuses offer students more options and more anonymity. There will be opportunities to develop a larger network of peers and to participate in a wider array of activities. Mid-sized campuses may also offer facilities, living arrangements, and opportunities for extra-curricular activities that smaller colleges do not. It is essential to know which activities are important to you so that you can look for them at colleges you visit.

Large universities are those with over 15,000 students. The mega universities boast 40,000 plus students. Their campuses are like small towns. Some of their campuses are larger than many small towns. They have their own stores, banks, and entertainment facilities. Residents who live near the campus often work at the university, look to the university for recreation, entertainment, education, and cultural exposure. Towns that are adjacent to large universities are fertile ground for service projects. Residents of these towns usually welcome the energy and passion of college students.

Large universities have larger classes and best serve those students who can advocate for themselves. Students in large lecture style classes need good note-taking skills and the ability to follow directions. At a large university, there are more opportunities to experiment with new interests, and due to the anonymity factor, the risks are minimal. As in a large city, there is much more to explore on a large college campus and innumerable resources.

Large universities are able to offer courses in every imaginable discipline. Financial resources permit these universities to plan frequent lectures by world-class authorities. They are able to bring in celebrated actors, musicians, artists, writers, political analysts, public servants, and anyone else that might enrich campus life. Internships, extracurricular activities, and service opportunities are endless and only limited by your time. What size school is right for you?

_____

_____

9. What kind of internships or special programs do you need?

_____

_____

_____

_____

10

Campus Culture

Student

The greatest contributor to emotional comfort, social acceptance, and access to opportunities is campus culture. Examine it carefully as you decide where to live and study. Just what is the culture of a campus? All organizations have cultures. Even your family has one. Culture represents the way the majority in a group has agreed to behave, live, and act. The group doesn't have a meeting to decide this, it just happens, usually by the influence of its leadership. Leadership on a college campus consists not only of adult administrators, but also of student leaders. Leaders may be elected or self-appointed. You've seen that before. The popular student, or most comical, or whatever other superlative seems to fit, decides to host a tailgate party at every football game. After a few games, other students join in and tailgating becomes part of the culture. This guy wasn't elected by anyone to start the parties; he just did it.

More often than not, students set the tone for a campus culture. Study habits (to have them or not), spiritual practice (church going or not), service projects (promoted or not), sports emphasis (jocks rule or not), weekend activities (jazz, classical, or heavy metal, or all of the above), fraternal organizations, (most students are in one or most students could not care less), internships/travel experiences (students are on the move or students stay put), student-initiated projects (all the rage or not), social life (tailgating or concerts), and so on.

Students who have developed autonomy are able to live happily anywhere, for they are frequently oblivious to what others are doing and thinking and are fully focused on their goals, interests, and ideals. They are usually able to find three or four other like-minded souls who share their interests, passions, or causes, and thus create a community of kindred spirits. Although some students are able to follow the beat of their own drumbeat and ignore the noise of the crowd, such independence is rare.

Compatible culture makes for a pleasant college experience and helps to create lasting valued memories. You see, when culture is compatible, you spend less time explaining yourself to people who do not understand and more time enjoying all of the wonderful things that the campus has to offer. If you are an independent thinker who works as well alone as you do with others and don't need to be included in a group to feel at home, the culture of a campus may not be important, but most people are group oriented.

Parents

It is impossible to have a real discussion about compatible campus cultures without looking closely at personal values. Some values are ingrained in students and will become a permanent part of their persona. Others were or will be discarded as students evolve into their own person. Don't be insulted or worried about this. You did not hold on to every thought and belief that your parents held dear and you are probably a better person because of it. Each person has to make his or her own way. Yet there are certain values that will remain forever.

If you look at the rate of transfers from one college to another after the first year, what you learn is that students frequently choose the wrong school to attend. A conservative estimate is that 41 percent of college freshmen either transfer to another school or drop out of college before receiving a degree. Some researchers estimate the number to be much higher. Sometimes the school is wrong because of the campus culture. Sometimes it is the location, instructional style, lack of resources at the school, lack of opportunities for creative expression, or any of a long list of other possibilities. Students later try to correct the mistake and frequently make a good choice. However, the financial cost of transferring to another college can be high and is something that could have been avoided.

The courses taken at one school may not be accepted at another. Requirements for graduation may differ from one school to another. Requirements for progress from freshman to sophomore year may differ from one school to another. Upon arrival at the new school, transfer students may have to pay to take courses they didn't expect to take, and they may not receive credit for courses already taken. What a bummer. Yet, it is worth the inconvenience just to arrive at the right place.

Some parents may be tempted to say that their child should jump in, get his feet wet, and either sink or swim. Remember, the student will be swimming in a pool of your money. You want to see some real swimming going on. The last thing that you need is to watch thousands of dollars sink. Students can sometimes go down faster than a big rock in a little pond and the experience can be devastating. Besides, who wants all of those late night calls from the lonesome dove complaining about the school, campus, professors, roommates, food, vending machines, how far apart the classes are...... You get the picture. Who needs it? Therefore, parents and students should take the time to look, visit, spend some time on campus, talk to students, and to use all of the investigative means at your disposal.

Student

It is so much better when you make the right decision and right selection in the first place. This requires paying attention and being honest about who you really are—not who you hope to be, or who others, including parents, want you to be-but who you are. I know of a young woman who received a full scholarship to study music at one of the Ivy League schools. She only lasted one semester. She received good grades, and she loved her professors. She grew tremendously as a musician, but she still left the school. She could not relate to the school culture. Her religious upbringing was so different from most of the students that she met. The social activities were shocking to this sheltered coed. Although the social interactions might not have surprised other students, she was appalled. If she had taken the time to spend a weekend on campus before enrolling, her decision might have been different. She had received numerous acceptance letters but instead of deciding based on personal values, she went for the big name, which is rarely the right way to choose.

The following questions will help you make better choices.

Seven Questions to help you discover the type of campus culture you need.

1. What do you need to feel at home?

_____

_____

_____

These needs can include activities, projects, service, spiritual growth, religious practice, groups to join, access to horses, or a chance to shine, or a chance to be a star. Some might be tempted to ignore this question and say that they can fit in anywhere. Maybe so, but do you think you will you be happy anywhere? Will you thrive, grow, reach your fullest potential, or be able to express all that you are? Some campuses have a sort of open culture where all students who want to participate in the campus life can do so. Others make students work a little harder to be in the mix of things. For the shy, less assertive student, a place like that will not work. For the student who does not enjoy working for a social life or who doesn't know how to work for a social life, aloof campuses will feel like a four-year sentence. What's right for you?

2. What kind of people do you enjoy?

_____

_____

_____

On some campuses, diversity is the rule of the day. Differences are more than tolerated. They are celebrated. However, I have actually visited other campuses where everyone looked like a clone of the last person. It just seemed that everyone adopted the same style of dress and speech, and the campus wide activities were similar. The students on these campuses prided themselves in being a homogeneous group. Yes, there are students who need and want a homogeneous campus (one where everyone is a cookie cutter image of the next). If you are off to college the right way, you want the chance to learn from the differences that you see in others. You will want to try different foods and different cultural activities and appreciate different art forms, worldviews, and political outlooks.

If you haven't figured it out yet, *Preparing for College Admissions* promotes diversity with as many varied experiences and opportunities to express and share talents as possible. The book also supports opportunities for the exchange of ideas with people from different backgrounds. College is the time to stretch and to grow. It does not mean that you supplant your own views with someone else's. It may mean that you will leave the campus at the end of four years with exactly the same opinions that you had upon entering. By then, you will know why you hold the opinions that you hold and will have at least listened to other points of view.

Do you appreciate political activity, like working on election campaigns for local or national offices, supporting causes of merit, even organized protest? Does that kind of thing energize you? If it does, look for that in the college of your choice. Some colleges feel electric with political activity. Yet on other campuses, students seem to be totally oblivious to the current political climate.

Expand the diversity notion beyond the political. Think about the activities that make you happy. Do you enjoy being in an arts environment where writers, poets, dancers, and musicians flourish, where it is common practice to attend a wine and cheese reception for an artist on Friday night and no one raises a brow, but asks you to tell them about it? Would you enjoy a campus where the Saturday night offerings vary from political debates to swim meets to theme parties?

3. Do you enjoy hanging out with the team, any team, more than anything else?

Some students need sports activity to feel alive. Others are only happy when the sports activity is part of some highly contested rivalry and occurs in a very public way. Of course, there are other auxiliary activities related to the sports environment like cheerleading, pep clubs, and parties. Sports provide great bonding experiences for new students and a way to share one's skills with others.

Sports activities can involve more than the campus group. They provide rich opportunities for service projects. Just think of the number of lonely children who could benefit from having a college student take them to a campus sports event. Think of the first generation college-going high school students who would be motivated to study harder after being invited to a college ball game. Those of you who feel the call to serve can find a way to do that and enjoy the games too.

Students who are involved in sports perform better academically because they must manage their time well in order to stay on the team. Most teams have grade point average requirements for participation, and that includes cheerleading. Frequently the passion for participation in the sport is the motivator to keep the grade point average high. Students find that time management and good organizational skills are essential to a successful school year. Busy students also find ways to access support services.

4. How important is spiritual practice to you?

_____

_____

_____

College campuses run the gamut from daily religious services and protocol for spiritual practice to no service or practice at all. Students must know their needs and recognize their commitments before leaving home. If a spiritual practice is important to you but it is non-existent on campus, where does that leave you? It is true that on many campus there are chapels, clergy, or at minimum bus transportation to places of worship. On others, there may be no resources for spiritual growth.

If the campus does not value spiritual practice, then it will not likely be a part of the campus culture. When a practice is not part of the local culture, it makes it more difficult for the student to participate. There will be little support or understanding for the student's spiritual needs. Some students need the opportunity for fellowship with other students of like mind. So, keep these thoughts at the forefront when you review brochures and when you make college visits. You should be forming a list now of questions for the admissions personnel when you meet with them.

5. In What kind of dorm would you feel most comfortable? Co-ed, single sex, theme oriented?

_____

_____

_____

Are there family values that should be considered? Colleges now offer so many different kinds of living arrangements. Parents may remember the old days of single sex dorms and two or three to a room. Well, that's another thing that has changed. Dormitories now are single sex, coed, organized by theme or interest. There are dormitories for athletes, for foreign language students, for various cultural and fraternal groups, and alcohol-free dorms. Yes, there are dorms where girls and boys spend the night in the same room whether it is the official policy or not. Look closely at the values that are important to you and determine whether the living arrangements at the college you are investigating will accommodate your needs and satisfy your values.

Students frequently go off to college thinking that everyone is just like them and that their values are common to the larger group. The first week of college can be a shock if students are not prepared for what they will experience. Students need to understand that when they arrive at college they will study and live with people from many different backgrounds. They might meet other students who have had experiences about which they have only read. This is why it is so important to be in a place where students can stay grounded in their own values while strengthening their own characters. Then, students are able to relate to a variety of worldviews without losing themselves.

6. Are you a loner or do you enjoy being with a group of people? What kind of group?

_____

_____

_____

7. What sort of activities do you enjoy doing alone?

_____

_____

_____

_____

In a group?

_____

_____

Why?_____

_____

_____

Carolyn Croom Baker

11

SELF-ADVOCACY

Student

Self-advocacy involves stepping up, stepping out, and seeking out those people who can help you to achieve your goals. In defining what you need in a college, consider campus services as well. Students from high schools where support services are minimal will be pleasantly surprised to discover the array of services in college. The following people are trained to help you achieve success in college: tutors, mentors, advisors, department chairs, professors, resident hall assistants, academic study center staff, support service staff for students with special needs, personal career development counseling staff, and many more. All of these people are there to support you.

Sometimes these people will put forth programs that are designed to support you and advertise them in such a way that they will be hard to miss. Other times, it will be up to you to locate and access the services that these people provide. Start developing self-advocacy skills in high school. High schools have a wealth of resources that go untapped by most students. They say that the squeaky wheel gets the grease. Well, learn to be the squeaky wheel. Tricia's mom will make sure that Tricia knows all of the right campus resources. Actually, Tricia started practicing in high school.

The best and most reliable way to find the truth about services is to talk to students on campus and personally visit campus resource centers. Information about support services will also appear in catalogues, brochures, and on the college's Web site.

1. When visiting campus resource centers, look for convenience of location, hours of operation, and quality of the staff. Are staff members trained professionals or just student assistants? I'm not knocking student assistants at all. Many of them make the best tutors. However, there are supports you may need that require a professional. Find out how easy or difficult it is to access the resource professionals at the college and just how comfortable they make you feel when you meet them. Comfort level will determine how frequently you use the services. Some students will avoid getting services they may desperately need just because access to them is too much of a hassle. Some people can tolerate more hassle than others can. At the price of most colleges today, why tolerate any at all?

2. Take a close look at the career services office. This resource can help you do a more effective analysis of your interests, passions, and aptitudes and help you determine the best career path. Career services personnel can also help you find internships, volunteer experiences, mentoring programs, and study-travel opportunities. Oftentimes, it is during an internship that a student will make a real commitment to a career path. Find out what their job placement rate is for graduates of the college. What sort of recruitment activity is there on campus for jobs during the college years and after graduation?

3. Look for service opportunities on or near campus. It is often in service or in the process of developing a service project that students discover their real life passion and purpose. It is truly an exciting moment when that happens. Start this practice in high school. Students who know that they want to go to college the right way quickly see the inherent value in service. The process of giving selflessly to others can bring your hearts alive with the passion to do more. Service also empowers you to see that you can affect change and see major results.

I have worked with a number of students who said that service projects turned their lives around, gave them courage, and built self-esteem. Some even said that service work opened the door to leadership experiences, which they would never have discovered on their own. There is no greater way to build lasting networks than to join hearts, minds, and energies to build something good. Students who work together on service projects remember their experiences for life, and they remember the team members who shared them.

Don't take these kinds of projects for granted. They contribute immeasurably to a resume that will make you proud and get you noticed. Students who want to contribute to society and find a way to do so impress universities and future employers. Seek out service opportunities in high school and college. It is a practice for life.

Students with Special Needs

Some colleges take pride in organizing support services to make them very easily accessible to students. Others have student support services with varying levels of quality. Again, the campus culture affects the treatment of students with special needs. It will also affect how comfortable students feel seeking help. Often it is the student without diagnosed special needs who requires support. Just as often, it is the honor student who accesses campus supports on a regular basis.

Eight questions to help you discover the kind of on-campus services you'll need.

1. Do you need opportunities for service projects and experiences? If so, what kind?

_____

_____

_____

2. Do you need opportunities for intercollegiate exchanges? If so, at which colleges or universities?

_____

_____

_____

3. Do you need opportunities for internships? If so, where are some of the places you'd like to do an internship? Why?

_____

_____

_____

4. Do you need opportunities for cultural exchange? If so, what kind?

_____

_____

_____

_____

5. Do you have a disability that will need accommodations? Do you need accommodations for your learning style? If so, what kind? (It will be helpful to refer to your current IEP, individual educational plan, or 504 if you have them.)

_____

_____

_____

_____

6. Do you need access to activities for spiritual development? If so, what kind? How often?

_____

_____

_____

_____

_____

7. Do you expect to need tutorial services? If so, in what subjects?

_____

_____

_____

_____

8. Will you need counseling services? Other mental health services? (If you do, be prepared to provide records from previous mental health service providers.)

_____

_____

_____

(Be as honest with this question as you can. You will want the college to be able to support your needs so you can achieve success.)

12

A Challenge To Greatness

Student

After you answer all of the questions about what you need from a college and how to advocate for those needs, consider this.

Leaving your comfort zone can catapult you into experiences that will make you great.

Challenge and some level of adversity also build character. With that in mind, choose a college that will stretch your intellect, help to uncover and develop your talents, and clarify purpose.

High school activities that involved taking academic or creative risks and seeking challenge, led you to this point. The right college accelerates the process of discovering the best that you are. The opportunities for personal growth will be unparalleled. The biggest job that you have right now is to choose that school that will both allow and invite you to stretch yourself.

Carolyn Croom Baker

Look for the college that will challenge you to learn more than you ever thought you could. Pay attention on your tours, visits, and overnights. Look for class arrangements including size, study challenges, access to professors, and activities that will help you grow and stretch your talents. Then, seek the college that will encourage you, nurture you, and provide a safe place for you to take frequent intellectual and creative risks. Look for a place where you are encouraged and supported while you explore questions and take the time to look deeply for answers.

Don't be seduced by designer labels, nationally recognized logos, winning teams (unless you are an athlete), or glitzy brochures. Those things won't get you educated the right way. Those things won't help you find the real you and your reason for being on this planet at this time in history. Those things won't make you the most informed, productive citizen that you can be.

I would encourage you to look for colleges that take pride in building leaders with character. This world desperately needs enlightened leaders who have faith in themselves and know how to encourage strength in others. Leadership qualities like that do not appear overnight. They have to be learned through experiences. So, the right college must provide numerous learning experiences through internships, cultural exchanges, international travel, intercollegiate exchanges, service projects, spiritual retreats and discussions, and other opportunities for personal expansion and character development.

The right college is different for every personality. We talked about that. This is a time when you will have to be as honest with yourself as you know how to be.

You will never reach your fullest potential in a place where everything is familiar and everything comes easily. It is true that you may thrive, even be happy, but will you discover all of the new and awesomely wonderful qualities that you possess?

Make a list of activities and educational experiences that you will try for the first time when you enter college.

Your college's catalogue and Web site will give you information about course offerings, student groups, cultural activities, internships and other learning opportunities.

New activities to try

_____

_____

_____

_____

New courses to take.

_____

_____

_____

_____

New groups to join

_____

_____

_____

A group or activity you would like to start. Why? Who will you seek to help you? What resources will you need?

_____

_____

13

COMMUNICATING WITH COLLEGES

Student

Congratulations! You have now successfully completed all of the questionnaires. With this information in hand, you are ready to contact the colleges of your choice.

You will need your notes to make a list of the eight or nine colleges that will be lucky enough to get an application from you. How do you sort through 4,000 colleges to find the eight or nine that are right for you? The truth is you will not have to do that. With good tools, you can navigate the maze with minimal effort.

Step 1: Use the Web to narrow your search.

Most high school guidance offices or school libraries have access to computer software that can help you narrow down your choices. Here is how it works. You input your name, other identifying information, preferences for college size, major, location, special interests, and any other criteria. The computer program will then give you a list of colleges that might be right for you. You have to do some work to determine the true quality of the list. A good test is to generate several lists from different sources and cross-reference them to see which colleges really stand out for you. If the same colleges come up on all lists, you know you have some winners. If you have a computer at home, great, but if not, you can use the local library or use one at school.

The College Board also has a Web site to streamline your search. First, you create a file on their Web site that you can access with a password. Then, you search for colleges. On the College Board site, you can input the criteria that are important to you, (like size, location, major, personal interests, student population) and generate a list of colleges for your review. From this same site, you can frequently link to the actual colleges and take a virtual tour. Your local librarian, school librarian, guidance counselor, or the computer lab instructor at your school can assist you.

There is also the Fast web, Peterson's Web site, the ACT (American College Testing Web site), Common Application, and other sites listed at the end of this book that can help you select the right colleges. The Common Application site can really help you fine-tune the process. It lets you see which colleges participate in the Common Application and from their site, you can link to all of the listed colleges. From the Fastweb site, you can access information about colleges and scholarships. You are selecting a home for the next four years, so start early and make this a leisurely effort. Early means start as soon as you begin to think about college.

Step 2: Request information from the colleges on your list.

Once you have a list, it's time to get in touch. This is what you do.

1. Stop at your local post office and get some plain post cards. If you decide to use the mail as your initial contact, the post card is the best way.

2. Address the postcard to the admissions office at the school you'd like to know more about.

3. Tell them that you would like an application, catalogue, and financial aid information. Tell them your name, address (with zip code), telephone number (with the area code), your prospective major, and any special interest you have, including sports.

4. The admissions office will put together a packet for you and may refer your name to appropriate department chairs or coaches. It's just that simple.

Do you remember the filing system we set up earlier? Get ready for the avalanche of mail. You have probably already started to get lots of mail that was generated by the PSAT questionnaire, SAT, or ACT exams.

If you want quicker responses, use e-mail. Most colleges have Web sites with the Web addresses of their admissions office and all other departments. If you have a computer at home, you can eliminate a few steps. You can access admissions offices whenever you want and whenever you have a new question. The admissions office can put you in touch with current students who may also e-mail you. If you do not have a computer at home, use the one at school or the public library. If your high school gives students individual e-mail addresses and passwords to access them, you can have the college contact you there.

Step 3: Meet with college recruiters.

High schools host recruiting sessions for college admissions officers throughout the school year. The guidance office, school library, and school career services office may alternate as hosts for college recruiting sessions. Pay attention, find out who is hosting, and go. Students from all grade levels may attend, but teachers are more willing to excuse juniors and seniors than younger students. Unfortunately, college admissions recruiters cannot always schedule their meetings during your lunch hour or after school. Most sessions are during the school day when you're in class.

These meetings are important for several reasons. Unlike at college fairs, you have the opportunity to meet with admissions officers in small groups. You will be able to get information, ask questions, and make an impression. Frequently, in these meetings, you will meet with the same college admissions officer who will review your application later.

The recruiting session is a great opportunity for you to ask questions about the campus culture, what students on the campus value, opportunities for service experiences, international travel, and access to spiritual development activities.

Tips on Meeting a College Recruiter:

1. Present your best self. First impressions last.

2. Introduce yourself if you can.

3. Shake hands and give direct eye contact.

4. Ask thoughtful questions.

5. Prepare a list of questions in advance of the meeting.

6. Sit up straight.

7. Take good notes.

8. Make sure that you fill out all forms carefully. Use black ink.

9. If you are interested in that college, ask the recruiter for his or her business card for your file.

10. If you are ready to put this college on your list, inform the recruiter that you will be in touch soon and ask about the best means of communication.

Here's another little known tip. Colleges keep track of the number of times you make contact with them. The e-mails, letters, face-to-face meetings in your high school, college fairs, campus visits, interviews, and meetings with alumni all add up to show levels of interest. In addition, these meetings will generate more mail for you. You will receive brochures, applications, pamphlets, and catalogues at these meetings along with business cards. As soon as you receive some-thing, put it in your book bag. Take all materials home to file or post.

Step 4: Tour the Campuses of colleges on your list.

Campus visits can be more fun than Disney World, or they can be one long pounding headache. I vote for the fun visit.

1. Take out your map of the United States. (If you are considering several colleges within the same state, you might need a map of that state.)

2. With a highlighter-ink pen, circle the towns that you plan to visit and draw a line from the first town to the next. The highlighter will make it easier to follow your travel plan.

3. Map out your visits according to your calendar of free time. When high schools are on spring or winter break, colleges are most likely in session.

4. Always call the campus before going. It makes for a better trip. College admissions personnel can arrange private or group tours for you, give you coupons to eat in the dining facilities free, and arrange interviews. They can connect you with freshmen who are majoring in your field of study, who can answer questions your tour guide cannot answer.

5. Visit schools in geographical order. It saves on gas and on stress.

6. Go on the Web site of the town or city where the college is located to find their local attractions. You might also be able to link from the college Web site to the town Web site and vice versa. You might luck out on some unexpected concert, natural wonder, or shopping opportunity that will add more fun to the trip. Shopping outlet developers love to locate in or near college towns. They are just waiting for you to shop and spend. (Be careful to save something for tuition!) The town's Web site can tell you about restaurants that serve the local cuisine. There may even be coupons for families visiting colleges.

7. Check with your local train station. Amtrak frequently offers reduced fares for

college touring. You might be able to visit several colleges with one train ride and save on gas. Bus companies may offer similar benefits. The college might also provide free transportation from the train, bus station, or airport.

College tour guides are pretty savvy. Most are current undergraduate students and many are on the work-study program. The money they earn from leading campus tours helps to pay for their tuition. They know the ins and outs, but there are things they will not be able to answer, either because they do not know or because it would be inappropriate for them to address your question. You may need to seek out others on campus to answer remaining questions or save them for the admissions officer.

Resort towns play host to more colleges than you might think. Vacations are perfect times to take a short excursion for a college look. If you don't like the school, you can always continue the fun part of your vacation.

Tours will run for about an hour, and on the tour, you will see classrooms, dormitories, sports facilities, dining facilities, libraries, and anything else the college wants you to see. The tour is designed to make you fall in love with the campus, not to show you its faults. However, if you attend that school, you will live with both the good and the bad.

Does this school interest you? Do you want to know more about the campus? Try these suggestions.

1. Talk to other students on campus.

2. While in line in the dining hall, strike up a conversation with another student. Find out what he or she knows and likes about the campus.

3. After the tour is over, wander off on your own and ask more questions of other students you meet.

4. If you are offered the opportunity to have an overnight visit, take it.

5. Some tours involve classroom visits. If they do, jump at the opportunity. Nothing will tell you more about how you will feel as a student on campus than sitting through a class or spending a night or weekend on campus. Notice class size, facilities, dormitories, and student support groups.

Take a private walk around campus.

1. Do you see students actively engaged in activities that interest you?

2. Are there good facilities to support your interests? For example, are there chapels, study centers, learning centers, or arts facilities?

3. If you are an artist, are there ample studios and practice rooms? Are they available to freshmen?

4. Does the Service Learning Coordinator have a presence on campus?

5. How active is the office for internships and cooperative work experiences?

6. How much international travel is going on?

7. How often do nationally and internationally recognized speakers and groups visit campus?

8. What kind of leadership opportunities might exist for you?

9. Is the campus population diverse?

10. Add to this list other qualities or resources that are important to you.

CAMPUS IMPRESSIONS

What I like about this campus.

_____
_____
_____
_____
_____

Issues I'd like to discuss further about this campus.

_____
_____
_____
_____

What I disliked about this campus.

_____
_____

On a scale of 1 to 10 with 10 being a real winner, how would you rate this college?

_____

Take detailed notes because after a while, all of the schools will start to blend. You want to remember the finer details when you get home. Take a few quiet moments to write your first impressions. First impressions sometimes tell the most truth.

Usually after the tour, you will have the opportunity to talk to someone in the admissions office and the financial aid office. If they do not offer this initially, ask for it when you call or e-mail to request the visit.

If you really like the school and think that this one might end up on your final list, let the admissions personnel know that you thoroughly enjoyed your visit. Be sure to send them a note or e-mail when you return home. That note becomes a recorded contact. If the admissions office provided any freebies for you such as rides to the station or airport, or free lunch or dinner passes, thank them. Everyone remembers nicely written thank-you notes long after other notes are forgotten.

14

Applying To College

Student

The application package consists of the application, the essay, letters of recommendation, transcripts, test scores, and other supporting documents. Technology has made the application process so much easier. Although you can still request hard copy applications to fill out and mail in, there are alternatives. **One of my favorite alternatives is the Common Application**. You can pick up a Common Application in the guidance office at your high school, in your school library, or at the local public library. You may also access the Common Application online.

College admissions officers have agreed to accept the Common Application, so don't let the name fool you. It is not common in the pejorative sense. It is merely common because a large number of colleges have agreed to use this form. When I last checked, there were several hundred colleges participating in the Common Application program. The colleges that participate accept the Common Application in the same way that they accept their own. The beauty of this application is that you fill it out one time and you are done. You can send the same application to any of the colleges on the list. Of course, you will have to pay the individual application fees or use a fee waiver, but at least you are cutting down on typing eight or nine individual applications.

Although a number of colleges accept the Common Application, some will ask students to complete a supplement to the Common Application. The supplement asks questions that provide additional information about the student. The supplement may ask for additional essays and other supporting documents. It is still more convenient to participate in the Common Application program than not. If you access the Common Application on line, you will be able to link to all of the participating colleges' Web sites to learn more. Go to **www.commonapp.org** for more details.

If you wish to apply to colleges that are not on the Common Application list, you will have to access their applications separately. Most colleges have Web sites, and their application for undergraduate admissions is generally on those sites. You can download them, fill them out, and mail them. Some colleges allow you to fill out your application right there on the computer and submit it online. The application fees and supporting documents can follow under separate cover.

Once you have the application, take great care with completing it. If you finish the application online, your work may be easier. The computer will keep it neat and clean.

Tips for completing your application.

1. If you are completing the application by hand, it will be helpful to make several copies of the application before filling it out.

2. Use one copy of the application as a dummy and fill in the answers to all of the questions.

3. Proofread it to make sure there are no errors.

4. Have another person proofread it to make sure it is error free.

5. Use a black pen to fill out the original copy of the application transcribing the wording from the dummy copy exactly.

6. If your handwriting is questionable, print. If the college wants to see your handwriting, they will let you know that.

After completing the college application, the real packaging begins. All of the things that we talked about in previous chapters will help you to package your application effectively. In the application package, you have the opportunity to showcase all the activities, service projects, honors, awards, and anything else that points to a young life well lived.

Take out all of the notes with the impressions that you entered over the years. Something in your notes may become a part of your college essay. You see, most colleges will want to see a writing sample and at the same time have another tool to get to know you better. The college essay is that tool.

Writing the Essay

Somewhere in the middle of the college application, after all of the identifying information and listing of activities, you will see questions that prompt the college essay. Some colleges are generous and give you general questions that allow you to use the same essay for other schools and purposes.

Try to begin working on your senior college essay in your English class. If you do, you will be a step ahead. Your English teacher can show you how to craft an essay that will engage the reader. Just think about it: the college admissions officer looks at hundreds, maybe thousands, of essays before he or she sees yours. Of course, if you really follow the instructions in this book, your application will be in long before the admissions officer becomes weary and his or her eyes start to burn.

TEN TIPS FOR CRAFTING A MEMORABLE WELL-WRITTEN ESSAY.

1. Start early.

2. Consider your audience. The goal is to let the admissions officer see how well you communicate. Write clearly, using standard English. The essay is a tool to help college admissions officers know you better.

3. Check grammar and spelling carefully. Your reader will appreciate a carefully and skillfully written essay.

4. Use 12-point type and no less or more than 1 ½-inch margins.

5. Use a simple font, Times New Roman or Arial, and be consistent.

6. Be original, but do not try to be cute or entertaining.

7. Write about a subject that you know well or a subject for which you have deep feelings. The best essay will come from a personal experience.

8. Limit your essay to a maximum of two typed pages.

9. When you finish the essay, read it aloud to see if it reads well. If you think it reads well, it is probably good.

10. Just to be sure, get three other people to read and critique your essay. Try to enlist the help of people who write well, like an English teacher, a neighbor who writes well, or a peer. Don't be too sensitive about their comments. Use them to craft the best essay you possibly can.

The high school guidance office supplies transcripts and copies of college entrance exam scores. You must also arrange to have scores sent from the College Board or ACT office to your colleges' admissions office.

Recommendation Letters

The letter of recommendation is the jewel in the college application package. It is like a testimonial, and it can sway the admissions decision in your favor. Handled badly, it can cause irreparable harm. A poorly written letter of recommendation can cause the admissions office to reject an applicant. You see, letters of recommendation can be positive or negative, and sometimes it is what is not said in the letter that does the most harm. Never try to force someone to write a letter for you. If the person you ask seems reluctant about writing the letter, or starts to give reasons for not being able to, politely accept his/her reasons, and ask someone else to write one for you.

1. Your high school guidance counselor will write one of your letters of recommendation.

2. You may request recommendations from teachers or from people you have worked with outside of school, including the supervisor of your service projects, supervisors from your civic or political work, or church officials.

3. Two of the three letters should come from current teachers, preferably those who teach in the area you plan to study.

4. Choose teachers who write and communicate well. More importantly, choose teachers who really like and respect you.

5. English, math, science, and history teachers probably receive more requests than other teachers do because everyone takes their subjects. Think about asking for a letter from a teacher in another area of study. If you have taken a number of art classes from the same teacher, consider asking that teacher for a letter of recommendation. You may have had several classes from the same foreign language teacher. That teacher may be able to write an interesting letter for you.

6. Make it as easy as possible for the teacher to comply with your request. The teacher will appreciate your thoughtfulness and might reflect that feeling in the letter.

7. Always give the teacher a stamped, addressed envelope for each college to which you are applying.

8. Provide a list of the colleges and their addresses in case one of the envelopes is lost.

9. If the college has its own teacher recommendation form, give it to the teacher with the addressed envelope for that school.

10. If the college has no form, give the teacher a copy of the teacher recommendation form in the Common Application as a guide. Some teachers will be new to the process and will appreciate some direction.

11. **When the recommendation is completed, say thank you and tell the teacher how much you appreciate his/her efforts.**

12. Write a short note to let the teacher know you appreciate his or her efforts. A nice thank you note goes a long way. You may need to approach the same teachers later in the year for scholarship recommendations.

Supporting Documents to include in your application packet if they are requested.

1. Newspaper articles that talk about your accomplishments.

2. Copies of special certificates or awards from school or civic groups.

3. Your creative writing samples that received special recognition or awards.

4. Slides of art projects from juried exhibits.

5. CDs of musical or theatrical performances.

When your application packet is complete, assemble the package with the college application on top, followed by the essay, letters of recommendation and supporting documents. Make a copy of the complete packet before mailing. You will save time in the future if you make multiple copies of your packet. File your copies to use with other applications to college and scholarship organizations. The guidance counselor will handle the remainder of the process. Guidance counselors will provide transcripts, counselor recommendations and available college entrance exam scores. You will still need to request official copies of SAT or ACT scores from the appropriate scoring agencies and ask that they be sent directly to the college.

Juniors and seniors, make a list of teachers you will ask for letters recommendation.

1._____

2._____

3._____

4._____

Always ask for more than you will need.

List supporting documents you already have.

1._____

2._____

3._____

4._____

5._____

List supporting documents you may still need if requested.

1._____

2._____

3._____

Make a note of SAT or ACT test dates

1.First test date:_____
Requested scores to be sent to the following colleges:

_____

_____

_____

_____

2.Second Test:_____
Requested scores to be sent to the following colleges:

_____

_____

_____

_____

3.SAT Subject Tests date:_____
Requested scores to be sent to the following colleges:

_____

_____

_____

_____

15

A Winner's Interview

Student

The interview is your time to put a face on the application. Many of the larger colleges do not host interviews due to the large number of students who apply and the strain on a staff whose energies are already stretched to the limits. Most large state universities do not encourage interviews due to staffing and time constraints.

However, small colleges and selective and competitive colleges encourage interviews because they need to get to know you. They want every available barometer to help them decide if you would be a good match for their college. The interview allows the admissions officer to see how well you communicate and how well you handle unexpected questions. It allows them to see your level of confidence, maturity, and genuine interest in the college. It allows them to ask you questions that the application didn't cover. Likewise, it allows you to ask questions and make a personal connection with the person who will have a great deal to say about whether or not you will be admitted.

Carolyn Croom Baker

Interview Spotlights

1. Spotlight your personal qualities, passions, interests, and values.

2. Use this time to talk about the things that are important to you and to your future. If you have been working on a service project, directing the school play, or involved in a church or civic project, the interview is the time to share the details, accomplishments, goals met, and lessons learned.

TIPS FOR A MEMORABLE INTERVIEW

1. **Always be your authentic self.** Yes, you want to make a good impression, and you want the interviewer to like you; however, you can't really control the attitudes of another person. You will never know what he or she really thinks or why. Ultimately, all you can do is put forth the best version of who you are and know that you and the "right college" will find each other.

2. **Prepare a few answers ahead of time.** Of course, you will never take out a piece of paper and look at your comments, but preparing a few answers in advance will give you time to think about what you will say. The admissions officer is going to ask you to talk about yourself. This is how they get to know you. Think about your best qualities and most interesting activities and be prepared to talk about them with positive energy. They may also ask you what you plan to study and why and how you will use your education in the future. Many interviewers will also ask about your weaknesses. They may ask you to describe your weakness or to tell them what you are doing to turn your weakness into a strength. Be prepared to talk about your strengths too. This is a difficult question for most people. Give it some thought before the interview. If it comes up, you will be ready with a well thought out answer.

3. **Prepare a set of questions.** Think of some thoughtful questions to ask the admissions officer. Compose questions that generate more than a yes or no response.

Try to think of questions that will generate an exchange of ideas. Maybe you could ask about the campus culture, what students value, or what seems most important to them. You could ask about faculty involvement in campus life, accessibility to professors, or student support services. You could ask about service projects and how to get involved, or about spiritual life programs and programs that encourage international exchange. You might also want to know about opportunities for leadership. Is it difficult to get involved on that campus or is everyone welcome? If you are an artist, you might want to ask about freshman access to the arts community.

4. **Review the notes you wrote during your campus visit.** If there is an aspect of the campus life that you are still unsure about, the interview is a good time to ask.

5. **Arrive on time.** Most admissions officers have a full schedule of interviews and won't appreciate lateness. Other students need attention. Keep your cell phone with you and the names and numbers of all admissions personnel. Call if it looks like you are lost or are going to be a little late. Be gracious if they allow you to come in late and thank them. Don't just walk in and start talking or act as if being late is no big deal. It is.

6. **Before going inside, turn off your cell phone.** Do not leave it on vibrate. Turn it off completely.

7. **Even though they will know who you are, introduce yourself and extend your hand for a solid — and I mean solid — handshake.** No limp fingers please. If you just left the bathroom and washed your hands, make sure that they are dry—desert dry.

8. **Keep eye contact from the beginning to the end of the interview.** Do not look at the ceiling, the floor, or the window, and never your watch. The answers are never there; they are in the eyes of the interviewer.

9. **Show interest in the interviewer's comments and try to engage him or her in a real conversation.** People like to feel that others are interested in them as well. Adults are no different from children.

10. **Ask about scholarship opportunities.** Although financial aid is handled in a different office, the admissions officer will know of opportunities that may help you

with the cost of your education.

11. **Never end the conversation yourself.** Let the interviewer tell you when the conversation is over.

12. **Express appreciation that the interviewer is taking the time to talk with you. When the interview is over, thank the interviewer, extend your hand for another handshake and make direct eye contact.** This will leave a final and lasting impression. Add a smile and make it a sincere one.

On–campus interviews are not always possible. If the college admissions officers still want to make personal contact, they may ask you to have an interview with local alumni. This can work very well for you. Oftentimes, alumni have more time to spend with you. Alumni do not have other students waiting outside their door. On the other hand, they may hold full-time demanding jobs and have only a few minutes. So, make the most of every minute.

Use this time to bring out your personal interests, things that you will commit to do, things that make your heart sing, things that you value. The alumnus will write a statement about you and submit it for your admission's file. That statement will be given as much weight as an on-campus interview.

Make sure that you find out how to contact the person who interviews you, whether that person is on campus or not. That person will become one of your allies if you stay in touch. So, stay in touch. Send a card to thank them for their time. Tell them again how much you appreciated the opportunity to talk with them. If this is a priority school for you, let them know that you would welcome the opportunity to meet with them again.

You may be invited for another one-on-one meeting or it could be a backyard barbeque with their family and other friends. Sometimes alumni host large events to connect prospective students with other alumni in the area. These are great opportunities for you to network. The alumni make mental and written notes about you and pass their thoughts on to the admissions office.

16

FINANCIAL AID MYTHS

Parents and Student

Today the average private college costs about $30,000 per year for tuition, room and board, and fees. By the time you add in travel costs, spending money, books, college fees, and laundry, the tab is more like $35,000. State supported colleges and community colleges are, of course, less expensive. Their costs are about half that of a private college or university.

For some students, the community college, state college, or state university is the absolute best choice. For others, it is the worst. As I mentioned earlier, the goal of this venture is to choose the best college for you, regardless of financial cost. Money should not be the overriding factor in making the decision. You will be surprised to know how easy it is to secure ample financial help for college tuition, and room and board.

So, when should you start? The key to the success of any project is early planning. Add to that good organization, focused and consistent effort, and you have a winning formula. Planning for financial aid and scholarships begins when you start to think about college admissions. Some parents begin at the birth of their child. O.K. You did not start exactly then, but you are starting now. If you started in the eighth grade or earlier, I applaud you. However, whether the student is in the eighth grade or a senior in high school, there are wonderful opportunities waiting.

You will need a pad, pen, some file folders, and post-its to start. Because you have a personal investment in the success of this venture, no one will be better at finding scholarship money than you. This project will demand the attention of parents and students. Everyone must remain wide-awake and aware of opportunities, because they show up in the strangest places.

First, let me dispel some myths about who qualifies for financial aid.

Myth #1: Only the really smart students can qualify for scholarships. Only the ones with straight A's should apply.

It is wonderful if you happen to be a straight A student, but just as many students with lower grades find support for their college dreams. Besides, here is a news flash for you: colleges do not even want to stack the freshman class with all A+ students. They want diversity in the student population. They want strong academically oriented students as well as serious students who will make the campus environment exciting by contributing to campus activities. Do you remember the discussion that we had about extracurricular activities and the benefits of service projects? Aside from the intrinsic value of these activities, there can be a payoff in the form of scholarships.

Myth #2: Only students with high SAT or ACT scores will qualify for scholarships.

High is a relative term. One college's high is another college's low. Different colleges have different standards for the college entrance exam scores. In fact, some very good colleges don't even require SAT or ACT scores. Imagine that. Princeton University no longer considers SAT or ACT scores the determining factor for admissions. It was never the all-important factor, but now it has even less significance. Scholarship donors recognize students for a variety of different reasons, not just test scores.

Myth #3: Teachers or school administrators must recommend students for scholarships or the student doesn't stand a chance.

It is a "feel good" moment when a teacher or school administrator recommends a child for an award or scholarship. Schools have access to a number of scholarships that generally come from local civic groups. The amounts vary from a few dollars to several thousand dollars. The qualifications can be anything from where a student attended middle school, to receiving high grades, to completing a number of volunteer hours. All kinds of criteria can be used to determine worthiness.

Sometimes donors approach school officials, counselors, or teachers to help them find worthy students for scholarships. When they do, counselors and teachers may seek out the most popular student, the most academic student, or the greatest athlete, depending on the criteria. The good news is that most scholarships and awards do not go through the school, and, therefore, school officials may not even know about these scholarships. Though some school librarians archive scholarship information, their archives may not include all of the available opportunities. What that means is there is money out there—other people's money—just waiting for you.

Myth #4: Students who have been subject to disciplinary action by their school cannot get scholarships.

If that myth were true, many very famous people would never have gotten through college. Unless you wave a banner that says, "I have been in trouble in school," who will know? Most people will not ask. If the offense had been that terrible, the school administration probably would have expelled you. If you are still in high school, your acts, no matter how foolish, have most likely been forgiven.

It is true that some scholarship application forms will ask if you have ever had any disciplinary action taken against you. You should tell the truth and try to explain the circumstances in the best light possible. If they don't ask, don't tell. School officials cannot reveal confidential information about you, including disciplinary issues, without your permission. Naturally, if you have a scholarship form that asks this question and you give it to your counselor to complete, he or she must answer truthfully. Your counselor may not, however, volunteer negative information. Records of disciplinary action are generally in your school record folder, but not on your transcript. Admissions personnel will only see your transcript and not your complete school record. Therefore, you are entitled to apply for everything that is appropriate to your skills and abilities. Nothing can hold you back. You are a winner. Remember!

Myth #5: Only the most popular students are chosen for scholarships.

There are thousands of scholarships that come from donors who know nothing about your school or community and who could not care less about who is popular and who is not. Donors give for a variety of reasons. Some set up scholarships in memory of their loved ones. If so, your qualifications for the scholarship may have to do with the interests of the dearly departed. For example, a parent may set up a scholarship in memory of a child who planned to attend college to study engineering. If you are also planning to study engineering in college, you are eligible to apply for the memorial scholarship. The parents may select you as the winner for a variety of reasons. You may remind them of their child in some way or express your goals in the same way. Donors may also represent large corporations that give to young people who patronize their businesses. Other donors may be recreational groups, national clubs, fraternal organizations, or even ethnic heritage groups. The list is endless.

Myth #6: You must hire a scholarship search company to help you find scholarships.

This is the biggest myth of all. I know a young woman, now a junior at Harvard, who secured all the money she would need to pay for tuition, books, room and board, and fees. She even found funding for extras: money for international travel, artistic projects, pizza, and trips home. She and her mother did all of this by spending just a few minutes a day paying attention to signs, posters, radio announcements, by scanning the Internet, and then, by applying to every available opportunity. There are even free college scholarship search sites on the Internet that you can access from your home computer, public library, or school library. The librarian will be glad to help you. (See the section of this guide titled "finding allies," pg. 47 for more details) Check the newspapers regularly, not just the large city papers, but also the little free neighborhood papers. People who want to give away money don't want to spend a lot of money informing the public that they have money to give, and they certainly don't want you to spend your money looking for them. Bottom line—check the neighborhood papers whenever a new issue is published.

> ****Caution**** By your high school sophomore year, you will be inundated with invitations to evening meetings in nearby hotels to discuss scholarships. The invitations say the meetings are free, and they are. But when you arrive, the promoters of the event will ask you to sign a contract for a fee. The promoters, who will bill themselves as financial aid consultants, will offer a guarantee to find enough scholarship money for you to cover the cost of the contract and even more. They are not lying to you. They will find some money, but they will use vehicles that you can easily access yourself. The goal here is to hold onto as much of your money as possible, so you have more money to help your child and more money to enjoy yourself after your child leaves the nest.

Myth #7: There are no scholarships for students with special needs.

Some parents believe that because their child has received, or is receiving, special education services, colleges will not be interested in their child, and, even worse, there will be no scholarship money for them. This is totally false. There is free money. There is private scholarship money, there are federal grants, and most states offer scholarships for students with special needs. State programs may also provide computers, visual aids, recording devices, and other supports. Step up and take advantage of it.

Special needs students are as multidimensional as other students are. They have gifts and talents that can be promoted to secure additional scholarship money or even to go to college free. Transcripts do not indicate special education services and neither do college entrance exam score reports. Therefore, the playing field is level. If you are a student who has worked hard, developed talents, or made special contributions to your community, there are donors who want to recognize your achievements with a scholarship.

Myth # 8: If you are just entering the game as a senior, you're too late.

Wrong again. It is never too late to aim for success. Some students and parents are under the misconception that if a student did not start developing a good reputation in the 9th or 10th grade, it is impossible to play catch up. **As long as you are alive and in school, you are still in the game.** Even if you are out of school, you are still in the game. Donors were once children, too. They, too, made mistakes, took education for granted, and at some point failed to appreciate all of the opportunities available to them. All adults can look back on their lives and see where they made a wrong turn or when they were not as productive as they could have been, yet they were able to set new directions.

If you are a senior who did not make the most of freshman, sophomore, or junior year, you still have opportunities. Your job is to make the most of what you know now, and let everyone know that you are doing just that. The good news is that you do know it now and understand the value of these opportunities.

People love to see someone come from behind and win. Remember the movies about the underdog, the guy who had all the strikes against him and then somehow, through inner strength, courage, commitment, or just sheer will, managed to overcome and surpass those who were originally out front. Success stories like this give us all courage and hope for our own futures. Donors want to support a young person who has had to overcome obstacles. Donors are people who are rooting for your success.

Myth #9: Parents who have no money saved should not even consider an expensive private college.

Suspend apprehensions about the cost of private colleges. Don't even consider price initially. Focus all of your energy and time on finding the college that will allow your child to become the fully actualized being that he or she was created to be and that you raised him or her to be. Think only about the qualities of the college, what they offer, what your child can gain from being there, what there is to learn, and what awesome experiences are available. Keep your focus on the college. Will it help your child to grow into a strong resilient, independent young adult who will make meaningful contributions to this world? Think about whether the college will provide experiences that will help your child to explore his God given talents to the fullest. That should be your focus, because someone really does have your back.

If you have no money and no way of getting any, don't believe anyone who tells you that your situation is hopeless or that your dreams for your child are unrealistic. You have these dreams because they were meant to manifest. There are numerous grants, scholarships and financial aid just for parents in your situation. Just choose the right school for the right reasons.

Myth # 10: Two working parents, middle-class parents, or parents with above average income will never qualify for scholarships or grants.

It's true that there are some financial aid programs for which you will not qualify because of your income. But the great news is that there are need-blind programs and merit programs that do not consider income or revenue sources. In fact, you will be amazed at the number of scholarship sources out there that are available and that do not ask about income. Students who have families who have worked hard and saved carefully do not have to be penalized. Help is there for you, too. Even if your child is not the star athlete or the featured tenor in the school choir, there is scholarship money for him or her, and this time you *will* spend it all in one place.

Students and parents can empower themselves to take financial matters into their own hands. They, in fact, have an obligation to do the best they can for themselves. Look for donors on posters in stores, eateries, shopping centers, and even bowling alleys. Did you know that there is a scholarship for students of parents who belong to bowling leagues, golf clubs, civic groups, certain churches or church organizations, fraternities, sororities, the Elks Lodges, the Masons, and for students whose parents work for companies too numerous to name? Take the power into your own hands and seek out these groups and others.

17

EARLY CASH FOR COLLEGE

Student

We have exploded the most talked about myths. There are others, but you get the point by now. Just throw out everything that you previously thought about funding a college education. Stay tuned for opportunities.

EIGHT TIPS TO CUT TUITION COSTS

Did you know that you could start making money for your college education while still in high school? If you want to go to college on other people's money, below are seven easy ways to do just that:

1. Take courses at your local college for free while you're in high school. Check with your guidance counselor. Many colleges allow high school students to take for free and for credit, the same courses college freshmen and sophomores are taking. Generally, you can enroll during your high school junior year; however, some colleges will not allow you to enroll until your senior year. Most colleges will limit your course load to one or two courses per semester.

Let's count credits. If you take even one course per semester free of charge and each course is worth three college credits, that's a total of six free credits by the end of your senior year. If you're able to enroll in junior year, you could possibly earn twelve free credits by the end of your senior year. What if you took two courses per semester? You can see how this computes over time.

Your PSAT, SAT, or ACT scores, along with your high school grades, will determine your eligibility to enroll in pre-college study programs. Colleges are looking for high school students who can handle the work and are mature enough to fit in with their college freshmen. I know of several colleges that allow high school seniors to spend the full second semester of their senior year on campus as full-time students free. Check with your guidance counselor to determine opportunities in your town. Since full time students take twelve to eighteen academic credits, consider how much money you would save. If you have fifteen college credits under your belt before entering college officially, you've already knocked off one semester of tuition costs. The good news is that you can transfer those credits to your future college.

If you are smart and take advantage of opportunities in your junior and senior year, free credits can really mount up. I am not suggesting that you give up your high school experience. You should continue to pursue a high school curriculum. Guidance counselors will adjust your schedule to accommodate your college classes. In most cases, you will take your college course first thing in the morning, and then attend high school later in the day, or the reverse can be true.

Students who take a full- time program during the second semester of senior year have to work a little harder to stay connected to their high school. College courses do not occupy the whole day every day like high school courses do. These students may still participate in high school extracurricular activities, sports programs, or music programs and may actually have more free time to participate in them than anticipated.

Although colleges that offer such programs want to attract top quality students, they do not require high school students who take courses on their campus to attend their college in the fall.

2. Take business or technology courses in high school that are aligned with local college courses. Responding to business needs, the U.S. Department of Education funded high school curricula changes to align certain business and technology courses with local college courses. Here is how this works: Businesses want high school graduates to be more prepared for the business world. So, in a collaborative partnership between businesses, local colleges, and high schools, backed by government funding, work-force-development courses were created in high schools to address business needs. These courses include computer science, marketing, accounting, business law, and a variety of other business courses. They are called "aligned courses". Check with your high school guidance counselor to find out which courses are considered aligned courses.

Aligned courses also include certain technology courses, such as computer graphics, computer programming, computer drafting, and other technology related courses. These courses have great transfer possibilities and also have built in moneymaking opportunities. I worked with a student who used his computer know-how to tutor senior citizens on computer use. This high school junior helped to put many grandparents in touch with their grandchildren who lived far from home. Because the courses were aligned with college courses, this student earned free college credit and also made good money tutoring the senior citizens.

You don't need to commit to a college major in business or technology to take advantage of this opportunity. Even if you plan to major in music or a foreign language or journalism, business and technology courses can help you accumulate credits. All colleges allow for electives outside of the major course of study in order to accumulate credits toward graduation. Through this process, you can enter freshman year with enough credits to qualify as a second-semester freshman or even a sophomore.

3. Enroll in Advanced Placement courses, as many as time permits. Not all high schools offer opportunities to take courses at a neighboring college or university.

If they don't, Advanced Placement (AP) courses are the next best thing. Meet with your high school guidance counselor who will review your transcript and current schedule to determine if AP is the right option for you. AP courses will be more challenging than your standard high school courses, but they are worth the effort. AP courses prepare you for the rigors of college. Once you complete the course, you will take an AP exam, a standardized test designed by the College Board. This test is given nationally to all students who complete an AP course. More good news: if you score well on the test, you may receive college credit for your efforts. That's right. You could receive even more free credits for college.

In order to earn the college credit, you must do well on the AP exam. Some students take a number of AP courses just to upgrade their transcript. It does help your transcript, but it doesn't save you money unless you take and do well on the AP exam.

4. Ask your guidance counselor for an application fee waiver. Along with rising college tuition costs, application fees have also taken a big leap upward. Many students can't pay the $40 and sometimes even $60 for college application fees. Multiply that by the eight colleges on your list. If you can't afford the application fees, ask your guidance counselor for fee waivers. The College Board supplies fee waivers for the college entrance exams, and they also supply a limited number of waivers for college application fees. There are nonprofit organizations in your town, some federally funded, that also supply application fee waivers. Simply attach these waivers to your application instead of a check, and the college will accept it. If your guidance counselor does not have access to fee waivers or does not know how to get them, ask the counselor to write one for you. He or she can simply write a short letter on school letterhead stating that the payment of the application fee will present a financial hardship for you and your family. The counselor signs the letter, and you attach it to your application.

Fee waivers shouldn't be abused. Don't use these waivers to send out twenty applications to colleges you know you will not attend. It is unfair to other students and some of the state universities will call you on it, but used with discretion, fee waivers are another great way to save money.

5. Sign up for courses at your community college. The tuition is lower, much lower, and community colleges frequently allow students to take courses for free while in high school. Even better, many will allow high school students to take free summer courses for credit as well. These courses will count toward graduation from a four-year college, particularly if you are planning to go to the state university.

Most students who aspire to attend competitive or selective colleges ignore the opportunities at the community college. Community colleges are supported by tax dollars and offer wonderful courses that are frequently taught by the same professors that the major flagship universities employ.

In addition, students who are not ready to leave home to attend college may find real value in taking courses at their community college. Such students can attend community college for a year or two and then transfer those credits to the state university, to a private university near home, or in another state. The tuition at the community college will be low, which means big savings, and students will have the opportunity to prepare for the larger world while living at home.

6. Get involved in cooperative work-study programs and paid internships. Co-op programs, or cooperative work-study programs, allow students to study for a few months, then go out and work for a few months so they can apply what they have learned. Two of the pioneers of this model, Antioch College in Yellow Springs, Ohio, and Northeastern University in Boston, Massachusetts offer students the opportunity to learn while earning money and developing an impressive resume at the same time.

There are numerous colleges that offer this kind of study plan, and it's a great way to save money. **The money you earn can be applied toward tuition or put into your pocket.** The choice is yours, depending on your financial arrangements with the college. Granted, traditional four-year colleges with the co-op plan often extend the expected graduation date to five years due to the amount of time off campus, but this doesn't have to be true for you. You could take required courses in the summer or add an additional course each semester and graduate in four years.

I worked with one very ambitious young woman who graduated with honors in three years from a co-op college. Cheryl wanted a college education, but her parents had no money. She had been a contributor to the family income while in high school, and as much as her family wanted her to go to college, they knew they'd miss her help. Her mother was divorced and disabled and there were two other younger siblings. Cheryl took care of the younger children in the evening, worked a part-time job in the afternoon, cooked the evening dinner, managed to do all of her homework, and still achieved honor grades while in high school. She knew that if she went to college, she would have to make every minute count. I helped her get all the money she would need for tuition, books, and room and board, but ambition and overwhelming responsibility caused her to kick it up a notch. Cheryl finished college in three years with honors. She also had an impressive resume from her many co-op experiences.

Paid internships can accomplish much the same goal. Internships put extra money in your pocket while you earn credits toward graduation and build a resume that will make you proud. Internships also help you define and refine your career goals.

7. Attend college year round and graduate in three years, saving a year of tuition. That may not sound like fun, but you'll discover that college is even more fun than high school, and you'll have much more free time. So, attend college in the summer while you're working your part-time job. You'll learn quickly how to multitask and manage your time. In three years, you will have earned your undergraduate degree and be ready for graduate school or the beginning of a great career.

8. Apply for an accelerated degree program. If you plan to attend graduate school or a professional school or just want to finish undergraduate school a little early, accelerated degree programs can shorten the time and cut the costs. Colleges are responding to students' demands for alternative, less costly routes to a college education. Therefore, some colleges are offering joint programs with professional schools of law, medicine, and pharmacy. Imagine graduating from medical school six or seven years after entering college, instead of the traditional eight years. Saving a year or two of college costs is sure to be good news to students and parents.

Policies for admission and for granting degrees differ from one college to another. If you are interested in this route, seek out more information from the college's admissions office. Be aware that most accelerated programs are extremely competitive. If you're up to the challenge, acceleration is a great way to save money and start your career early.

18

FINANCIAL AID

Work For Parents and Student

Financial aid is an umbrella term used to describe a variety of financial supports for college students. Students who have absolutely no money and no resources can benefit tremendously from financial aid. However, quiet as it is kept, middle-class students with two income-producing parents can benefit from financial aid as well.

Remember that the average private college education ranges in cost from $30,000 to $40,000 annually. A four-year education is currently the biggest investment you'll make, next to purchasing a house. A college education now costs from $120,000 to $160,000. Knowing that, you can see why so many students will be eligible for financial aid. How many people can actually write a check for $30,000 for four consecutive years? Not many. Unless colleges are interested in preserving a population of only the very rich, they must design ways to help students from varied economic backgrounds attend. Most colleges want to have a diverse population. It is no longer like the old days when only the rich could afford to go to college, and the poorer students worked their way through by scrubbing the floors, tending the lawns, and serving the needs of their wealthy peers. Today, all students can attend college and do it with dignity. Students simply need to take advantage of all the available resources.

Please keep in mind that the financial aid process is not a mystery that only a few can understand. It is not necessary to pay some high priced consultant thousands of dollars to find aid for you. It is there waiting for you to claim it after just a few simple steps.

First, let's look at the components of financial aid. Just what is it and where does it come from? Financial aid comes from institutional money, state money, and federal money:

INSTITUTIONAL MONEY

This block of money comes from generous donations from alumni, corporate friends, and plain citizens who believe in supporting the college's programs. I once read of a single working woman who lived a very frugal, simple life. The woman had no heirs. When she died, her will stated that all of her money would go to the nearby Ivy League college for scholarships. You see, even though this woman was not an alumna of the college, she had always dreamed of being able to attend a college like that. She thought that she could at least pay the tuition for some other child who shared her dream. Colleges and universities maintain millions of dollars in institutional money, and they are constantly replenishing their coffers.

FEDERAL MONEY

Included in the federal pot are federal grants, loans, and work-study programs. Scratch the idea that federal financial aid is only for the very poor. It will help the very poor, but it can also help the middle class and even some people who are a bit above middle class. This is how it works. Most colleges are committed to having a diverse population. That means they want students of all economic backgrounds. No longer is college for the convertible driving, fur coat-wearing student whose parents practically invented money. Higher education is for everyone. So what does that mean? In order to attract low to middle-income students, colleges must offer financial aid. They know that they cannot attract poor and middle class students by telling their parents that they will have to raise more than $30,000 for their child's college education.

All colleges and universities have an office of financial aid, and this office amasses large sums of money from various sources just to help you and your family make your dreams real. Imagine that! In most cases, the admissions office and financial aid office operate separately.

TYPES OF FEDERAL MONEY

1. **Pell Grants.** The maximum Pell Grant amount varies from year to year, but it is currently around $4,000 per year for undergraduate students. You may apply for this grant each year of undergraduate study, and it doesn't have to be repaid. Need is the only consideration for this grant. Grades and college entrance exam scores are a non-issue. Students who are U.S. citizens or permanent resident aliens may apply.

2. **Supplemental Educational Opportunity Grants (SEOG).** The SEOG also does not have to be repaid. You can receive up to $4,000 per year for undergraduate study. Students who are U.S. citizens or permanent resident aliens may apply.

3. **Perkins Loan.** You may borrow up to $4,000 per year, not to exceed $20,000, for your total undergraduate education, with a 5% fixed interest rate. The interest rate may vary from year to year, but once the loan is in effect, the interest rate remains stable. The government pays the interest while you are in college. Repayment doesn't start until you've graduated from college. If you attend graduate or professional school after earning your undergraduate degree, repayment is postponed. Financial need is a determining factor.

4. Subsidized Stafford Loan. Students may borrow a total of $23,000 for undergraduate study. The interest rate is a little higher, and financial need determines the amount that can be borrowed. The government pays the interest while you are in college.

5. Unsubsidized Stafford Loan. Dependent students may borrow up to $23,000 while in undergraduate school. Independent students—students who no longer live with their parents and who are not claimed on the parent's income tax forms—may borrow up to $46,000 for undergraduate education. **Since the federal government does not subsidize this loan, students MUST pay the interest on this loan while in college.** An application form can be found at your local bank.

6. Plus Loan. Parents who wish to borrow to help pay for their child's education may choose to use this vehicle. The PLUS loan has a variable interest rate, which may or may not be higher than the interest rate on a home equity loan. Parents who own their own home may want to investigate a home equity loan to pay for college. PLUS applications can be picked up at your local bank.

7. Federal Work Study. The college financial aid office will help you find a job on campus for a few hours per week. The money that you earn is used to offset the expense of your education. This experience will also strengthen your resume.

Don't be afraid of college work-study programs. Students who participate in the work-study program only work ten to fifteen hours per week, and they are generally placed in jobs that are related to their major. One student that I know wants to be a journalist, so she works doing research for a professor who is writing a book. Her research is related to another one of her interests, women's studies. She is thrilled with the opportunity and gaining valuable experience that will look good on a future resume. She will also get a good recommendation from the professor for her hard work.

I have issued cautions before about high priced consultants who make outrageous claims about what they can do for you and how much federal money they can help you get. Heed them. You really can handle this process on your own and if you get stuck (and I don't think you will, but if you do), you can call on the financial aid office at your local university or see the guidance counselor at your child's school. There are also federally funded programs in each state that will offer free consulting services for the financial aid process. So do the work yourself. Hold on to your wallets, and use those consulting fees for your child's education. You will be pleasantly surprised at how easy it is. Don't worry that you might miss something. If you miss a question, the processing center staff will let you know. So let's get started.

APPLYING FOR FINANCIAL AID

1. Get your hands on the Free Application for Federal Student Aid. also known as the **FAFSA, by December of your senior year.**

You can find the FAFSA at local colleges, libraries, and the offices of federally funded financial aid assistance programs. Based on the answers you provide on the FAFSA, the college financial aid officer will decide how much financial aid you will need. If you log on to www.studentaid.ed.gov or the United States Department of Education's Web site, you will get all kinds of information about the FAFSA. Below are tips for filling out the **FAFSA**. Students and parents will need to work on this.

2. Apply Early. Colleges have a finite amount of money that they can distribute for financial aid. I have seen some unfortunate students who waited until the last minute (sometime in March) to file financial aid forms, only to discover that the college had no more money to distribute. You, however, will not have that problem, because you will start early. Your FAFSA will be mailed to the processing center immediately after January 1. Do not mail the application before January 1 or it will be returned. The idea is to mail it as soon after January 1 as possible.

The FAFSA gives instructions on how to file online. It is actually the preferred route. It is faster, and there is no chance of it getting lost in the mail. You get a PIN number that allows you to access your information and to be notified if there are any necessary changes or additions.

Also go to *www.studentaid.gov*, and you will find what you need to file. On that Web site, you will also find valuable information about college admissions, scholarships, grants, college applications, and other tidbits. Your government has really stepped up to the plate. The information they provide is useful and helpful. The doublespeak is almost nonexistent. If you prefer, you may also go to **www.fafsa.gov** to file online. Do that and you will be on time, right up front where you and your child belong. When Tricia's mom arrives, you'll be there to greet her.

3. **Have on hand the following documents when completing the FAFSA:**

   a. Your Tax forms, (IRS 1040 or whatever form you use). I know this means you will have to get started early preparing your income tax process, (and who wants to face that), but you must. The **FAFSA** will ask questions that require you to pull information from your tax form, but you don't need a completed tax form to fill out the FAFSA. You can use the last paycheck you received in December. That check usually summarizes your income for the year and taxes paid. Your W2 will arrive before the end of January, and it, too, has valuable information that you can use. You can also make projections from last year's tax return.

   b. Records of unusual expenses, for example, care for an elderly parent, catastrophic acts of nature, repairs to your home, medical emergency expenses, or anything that has siphoned off your financial resources. If you have other children in college or private school, there is a place to report that information. If you are paying tuition for yourself or your spouse, that expense decreases your expendable income and should be reported. It will mean more money for your child.

   c. Income verification for both parents and students. You will all need social security numbers, income statements (if you are not employed), and W2's to complete the process.

   d. Records of investments for parents and students, Include records of savings accounts, real estate, trusts, and any other income sources.

e. The College Scholarship Service Profile, also known as the CSS Profile, This is another financial reporting form. Many private colleges require this form and may require that you complete their institutional financial aid form as well. The CSS Profile should be completed early in your senior year. It is available in your high school guidance office or online. The CSS Profile is an important part of the financial aid process, so get it and do it quickly.

4. Complete the FAFSA carefully, in black ink or online, and do not leave anything blank! Make a few copies of the blank FAFSA and rough out the information on the copy first before transferring data to the original application. This can be quite helpful when applying online.

5. Tell the truth about your financial status. The financial aid office operates autonomously from the admissions office. Your child will not jeopardize their candidacy by being "too needy".

6. If parents are divorced, the custodial parent's income is primary. Child support is always included in the income of the custodial parent. Be aware that some colleges will ask for the non-custodial parent's income information.

7. Independent students file their own FAFSA. Students who live alone and who are not claimed by their parents on the parents' income tax reports are considered independent students. There are local agencies that help independent students file, and representatives from those agencies or from the college financial aid office will be able to provide detailed information about independent student filing policies.

8. Early decision colleges may ask you to complete their own institutional form to determine financial aid. Students who file an early decision application to college will apply to college by November 15 and will be notified of admission by December 15. Some colleges may ask for early decision applications by October 15. Therefore, the college will not be able to review your FAFSA until after you receive your letter of acceptance.

STATE MONEY

Each state makes provisions for the education of its students. There are state grants for students that are issued based on grades and college entrance exam scores. Students may access applications for state grants through their high school guidance office. In some cases, there is no application. High school guidance counselors simply turn in the names of students at the top of the class who qualify for the grant.

Each state allocates money for higher education differently. If you contact your state office of higher education, you can find out what your state has to offer. After all, your tax dollars fund your state's colleges as well as special scholarships for state residents. The state is invested in having well educated citizens because they attracts big business, and big business generates big tax revenues for the state. I'll bet you didn't even know how important you are to your state. If you don't grow, the state stands still. So grow!

States offer grants to graduating seniors in varying amounts. Grants awarded to high achievers provide needed support with no repayment obligation. Some states offer grants for students who major in areas that are needed by the state; these grants also do not have to be repaid, provided the student works in that field for a pre-determined time.

States also offer a variety of student loans. The lower interest rates go to the neediest students. State supported incentive programs, usually in the form of tax credits and special loan interest structures, encourage saving early for college. Again, your state's office of higher education, department of education, or education policy staff in your governor's office has information about the different opportunities available.

There are state grants for students who plan to attend college within their state. If you and your parents determine that a college in your state is the best choice for your goals, a state grant can be a welcome addition to the college fund. There are also separate grants in some states for students who plan to attend the state's public colleges, community colleges, and universities. Your high school guidance counselor would be the person to direct this process. Ask your high school guidance counselor for the application or information about such programs. If your counselor does not know, be sure to talk to the financial aid counselor at the college you hope to attend. College financial aid counselors can be very helpful in the whole financial aid process, and they are quite generous with their time. Like federal grants, state grants do not have to be repaid.

PRIVATE MONEY

Then there is private money. That's right. There is free money that is not tied to any governmental structure, and it is waiting for you. It too comes in a variety of forms:

National Merit Scholarships

If your score on the Preliminary Scholastic Aptitude Test: National Merit Qualifying Exam is high, you can receive one of the National Merit Scholarships. Your PSAT results will determine the outcomes. You must take the National Merit Qualifying Exam in your high school junior year. Of course, you may and should take the exam earlier than junior year, just for practice; however, only the scores from your junior year will count towards the scholarship. Colleges all over the country will be notified of the National Merit Scholarship winners and Commended Scholars. Those students may receive scholarship offers from interested colleges. National Merit Scholars will receive $2500.00 awards. They may also receive awards from interested members of the corporate sector. For more information about this important scholarship, go to **www.nationalmerit.org**.

Arts Recognition and Talent Search Scholarships

Artistically talented students, including visual artists, musicians, dancers, actors, and writers, may apply for the Arts Recognition and Talent Search Scholarship. This is sort of an SAT for artists. Go to the Web site for Arts Recognition and Talent Search to look at the application criteria. This scholarship is substantial, and not as many students apply as you might think. If you have recognized talent, make sure that you take advantage of this scholarship. Colleges with recognized arts programs are notified of students who perform well.

Local Philanthropy

- Local civic, fraternal, church, and educational groups as well as various nonprofits and even private individuals are interested in rewarding you for your accomplishments. These groups are small and generally do not have a large advertising budget to let the public know that they're out there. For example, a church may make an announcement during service and not publish the notice anywhere or your bowling league may only post an announcement at the bowling alley. Fraternal organizations and social clubs may make an announcement through their membership. So you have to seek them out.

- Notices about scholarships and awards can be found in the public library, in public service announcements on the radio and television, in small newspaper articles, listed on flyers at school, posted on the bulletin board in the guidance counselor's office, or in the school library. Some school districts distribute a scholarship publication printed by a local non-profit or business.

- The police department and fire department offer scholarships in many towns for students who are contributing to the life of the community. Even political figures offer scholarships. If you have actively volunteered to serve your community, there may be a scholarship out there for you.

- Check the offices of your mayor, congressional representatives from your district, state representatives, and other local politicians who might have access to scholarship information for you.

- Many cities and towns have a designated community organization that serves as the channel for grants to nonprofits as well as scholarships to young college age students. It is sometimes called a Community Foundation, though it may have another name. Organizations like this would be familiar to the public librarian. They probably publish a booklet of scholarship information.

Sit down right now and make a list of every organization that might offer you a scholarship. Don't leave anyone out. Research the names and contact numbers of potential donors and note them on your list.

Include all of the clubs and organizations to which you belong including service organizations, church groups, civic groups, hobby groups, social clubs, and athletic groups. Include your employer and your parents' employer. Write down all the places where you do business. Write down the names of your local newspapers, radio station, department stores, fast-food eateries, golf courses, bowling alleys, swim clubs, tennis clubs, and ski clubs.

Potential Scholarship Opportunities

Athletic Groups

1._____

2._____

3._____

Businesses You Patronize

1._____

2._____

3._____

4._____

Civic and Service Organizations

1._____

2._____

3._____

4._____

Cultural Activities

1._____

2._____

Favorite Eateries

1._____

2._____

3._____

Favorite Family Snacks

1._____

2._____

3._____

4._____

Fraternal Organizations: Mom, Dad

1._____

2._____

Local Media: Newspaper, Radio, Television

1._____

2._____

3._____

My Club Memberships

1._____

2._____

3._____

My Employer

1._____

Parents' Club Memberships

1._____

2._____

3._____

4._____

Parents' Employer

1._____

2._____

Religious Groups

1. _____

2. _____

3. _____

Stores You Frequent

1. _____

2. _____

3. _____

Talents

1. _____

2. _____

3. _____

Places You Go for Recreation or Fun

1. _____

2. _____

3. _____

Charge Cards

1. _____

2. _____

3. _____

Now go back over your list and see if you can think of others.

1._____

2._____

3._____

4._____

Look at the items you buy at the grocer's. The snack bags, soft drink bottles, or cookie bags may hold a clue. **Did you know that Coca Cola offers a scholarship for students who have been actively involved in improving the community?** You must be relentless about this. It's not a full-time job. It will not absorb all your time. You simply begin to see your world in a new way. You will see opportunities where you used to see just more places to spend money. While we're talking about spending money, look at your charge cards. **Did you know that Discover Card offers a scholarship to juniors** who are college bound? Who would have thought it? If Discover Card offers something, and it's a good size award, don't you think other charge card companies might offer a scholarship,too?

Let your mouse lead the way

I have listed a number of internet resources at the end of this book. A few of them can really put you on the right path to financial help. FASTWEB.com is one of my favorites. It is free, easy to use, and if you have a computer at home, they will email you regularly with updated information about scholarship opportunities. If you do not have a computer at home, you will have a password to use at school or in the library.

All you have to do to access this resource is Google FASTWEB. There is probably information about this Web site in your school guidance office. You will enter your personal identifying information to set up an account. Tell them what you plan to study, something about your interests, and answer a few other simple questions. That's it. Then, as often as you'd like, you can go to that site and check out new opportunities. Keep a record of all resources you discover with names, deadline dates, and appropriate contact information. Follow up on all resources.

I want you to be as good at finding money for college as the IRS is in April. The key is to start early. The farmer who starts early can expect a much larger harvest than the one who waits until summer to plant seed. So start planting!

HOW NEED IS DETERMINED

At the processing center, the financial aid analysts look at all of your information, crunch all the numbers, and then determine how much money they think you should be able to spend on your child's education. That amount will be referred to as the EFC, Expected Family Contribution. That amount will be reported to you in your SAR, Student Aid Report. You and the college that your child hopes to enter will receive the SAR about three weeks after you file the FAFSA. If you file online, you will receive the SAR online and can access it with a PIN number. The report will not be sent out until the analysts are sure that all the information is correct.

The college then reviews your report and compares it to the total cost of attending their school, which includes the cost of tuition and room and board. **The difference between the EFC amount and the total cost of attending the college is your demonstrated need.** As soon as your demonstrated need is determined, the college financial aid officers go to work. They will look at all of the sources of money they have and decide how much they can allocate for your child's education, your child's future.

Now here is another very important point to consider and consider well. Some colleges state in their promotional material that they will meet 100% of a student's demonstrated need. If they do, you will not have a financial gap when your child enters college. Others will tell you that they will only meet 80% or even 75% of a student's demonstrated need. Now what does all of this mean? A college that will meet only 75% of a child's need may leave you with a financial gap that will be difficult to fill unless you plan for it. Keep in mind that any money the student earns during the summer has already been calculated in the formula to determine need, since the college expects that the prospective student will work during the summer. So, summer earnings will not help to fill a financial gap. Read your college's promotional materials carefully. They will thoroughly explain financial aid policies.

Some colleges give more grants than loans, and other colleges issue more loans than grants. You do not have to repay grants. Loans, of course, must be repaid, although conditions for repayment may differ depending on your child's financial status. Colleges may not exactly spell this out for you. It doesn't make for good advertising copy. You must pay close attention to what they say and to what they don't say. **You definitely do not want to end up with a loan the size of a mortgage at the end of four years. If that happens, what about graduate school? More loans?**

Be aware of the colleges that subtract private scholarships you received from the full amount of the financial aid package. What happens is this. Let's say you follow all of the advice given in "Finding Financial Allies", and you get several different scholarships from a number of local and national sources totaling about $8,000. Let's say you qualified for $20,000 in financial aid from the college. Your scholarship sources have nothing to do with the college or that college's financial aid process. However, if the donors send the money to the college bursar instead of giving it to you, many colleges will subtract that $8,000 from the financial aid award, (from the $20,000, they were planning to offer you.) In this case, the college's financial aid award may be reduced to $12,000, and the $8,000 you worked so hard for will be swallowed up in the financial aid package. Sometimes, you just can't get around this policy. However, there are colleges that don't follow this practice and take the position that if you earned the money, you get to keep it. If the college does include private scholarship money in figuring your financial aid package, try to get them to subtract your scholarship money from the loan part of your package, which will reduce your total debt by the end of the four years.

YOUR FINANCIAL AID AWARD NOTIFICATION

Financial aid award letters will come at different times depending on the notification policies of the college. Here is what happens. As soon as the admissions office makes a decision, they notify the financial aid office. Financial aid officers look at the full list of admitted students and start to "package" each student for financial aid. They look at the total need that each student has. Do you remember the **EFC** and the **SAR** that we talked about earlier? Financial aid officers look at what the EFC (Expected Family Contribution) says the family can pay. They then look at the cost of attending their college. They subtract the amount the family can pay from the total college budget for one year, and that amount becomes the need. Financial aid officers then put together a package for the student. The package, comprised of college grants, federal grants, loans, and work-study, will become a part of the **Financial Aid Award Letter.**

The award letter will frequently arrive along with the admissions letter. It can also come under separate cover, but it will be very close to the arrival of the admissions letter. If the college to which you are applying has a policy of **rolling admissions, students will be admitted as they apply**, and financial aid offices will mail award letters accordingly. Sometimes, there is a delay between the time the admissions letter arrives and the arrival of the award letter to the home of the prospective student. **Other colleges wait until all admissions applications are received.** Then they review all of the applications together and make a decision by the first part of April. Students will receive notification from the admissions office and the financial aid office by April 15. Students will then be instructed to make a decision and respond to the admissions office and include a dormitory room deposit by May 1. This will give the family two weeks to review the admissions letter and the financial aid award letter to determine if the offer is one that will work for them.

It is important to review the components of the financial aid award carefully. Look carefully at the loan to grant ratio. I have seen some unsuspecting parents review the financial aid award letter much too casually. Some parents look at the bottom line—the total figure—and start rejoicing over the large amount of money their child will receive, when a closer analysis might reveal that most of the award is loans, which must be repaid. **REVIEW ALL AWARD LETTERS CAREFULLY BEFORE HAVING THE PARTY**. An admission to college is a good reason to celebrate, but make sure you understand what it will cost the family.

HERE'S A CHECK LIST FOR REVIEWING YOUR AWARD LETTERS.

1. **Make a list of all private scholarships you've received**, and make sure that those scholarships have accounted for all gaps in your financial aid. You should now have sufficient money to cover the dream.

2. **If you find that you still have a gap between what it will cost to attend college and the money you have actually received, most states have resources to help with financial gaps.** These resources are frequently entitled **Gap Programs**. Students who have completed service projects or who have been active in their community can contact the organizations for which they worked and ask for support. If the organization cannot fill the gap, they may be able to fill part of it or refer you to someone who can help. Remember to include these organizations on your list of allies.

3. **If you still have a few hundred dollars of gap left**, divide the total amount into small bits and ask businesses in your area if you can apply for a scholarship in that amount. Remember that everyone in your town and everyone that you meet is a possible ally to help make your dreams real.

4. **For the very talented,** Cooper Union College in New York and Curtis Institute in Pennsylvania provide a free education for any student who is admitted. Berea College in Kentucky offers a variety of majors and only admits students in need. All students attend tuition free. There are others; search the Web addresses provided at the end of this book to flush those out.

If you follow all of the advice in this book to the letter, you will reach your goals. What you discover on this journey will teach you lessons about your own resourcefulness that will serve you well in the future. You and your parents will create precious memories, save money and secure your future. Both you and your parents will be able to enjoy life after high school.

The next section is all about staying safe once you enter the college of your choice. I hope you will read it carefully and consider implementing the suggestions while in high school. Yesterday, I received an email from a former college coed who didn't heed the advice in the next section. Her life has been altered beyond measure. College is no longer part of her reality. She will need a long time to recover from the trauma she experienced one lonely night in a deserted park.

You worked hard to achieve your goals. Protect them. Stay safe.

19

STAYING SAFE

Parents

Students' decision-making skills are too often less developed than their academic skills. This is where you can be a big help and may be able to save your child's life. I recently spoke with the president of a small prestigious liberal arts college. He said that as parents prepare students for the college experience, they should caution their youngsters particularly about appropriate conduct and safety. Young people so easily feel immortal and invincible. Students who come from homes and communities where most people can be trusted enter college trusting everyone, including untrustworthy strangers. So, I decided to include this section on safety because it is so important.

The college president told a story about a bright young woman who entered his college on a merit scholarship. She planned to study history and politics. Her parents did not think to caution her about leaving campus with strangers. She thought that everyone was just like her family and friends. She was also a bit strong willed and did not heed the advice of the residence hall staff. You see, the residence hall at this college was in a large tourist-attracting city. Although the college was in a safe and lovely residential section of town, the city was home to all kinds of predators.

After she had been on campus only two weeks, a young man driving a convertible stopped in front of her residence hall and offered the young coed a city tour. She thought that he seemed nice and friendly. Against the advice of friends, she accepted his offer. She was returned to the residence hall 24 hours later beaten and raped, with no identification or wallet. So much was taken from this young woman in those 24 hours that can never be recovered or replaced.

Not too long ago, families watched in horror the nightly news tale of the young woman who went to Aruba with classmates to celebrate her graduation. She, too, trusted the wrong strangers. She, too, failed to heed the advice of her friends. The results were devastating to family, friends, and to a whole nation of news viewers who empathized with the resulting tragedy. Then, there was the young intern in Washington, D.C. who met tragedy in Rock Creek Park. I could continue with other examples but you have seen those on your local news stations.

It is so easy to think that these incidents are isolated occurrences. According to one college president, they happen more frequently than we would like to think. He said that when he meets with his colleagues, student safety is a major topic of discussion not because campus security is a big problem, but because many students come to college before they have matured into young adults who make wiser choices.

Student

High school is the time to start building a safety practice for the future. You can establish habits in high school that will carry you successfully and safely through college.

Here are 12 safety rules that will help to protect you and your future. Start practicing them today.

1. **Tell your parents or someone in your residence hall where you are going and with whom, particularly if you are leaving after dark.** It is always important to let people know when you leave and when you are coming back. When you live in a dormitory, tell a neighbor or resident assistant where you are going. If no one is around, leave a note on your desk. Please start this practice in high school. Never leave home without informing others about your destination and with whom you will spend your time. Safety and secrets are not compatible.

2. **Hang out in groups.** Young people frequently welcome strangers into their plans and activities. That's great. That's a fine way to meet new friends. However, while getting to know the new person, it is so much better to build a safety net of friends. Travel in groups of four to eight friends, people you know well. Bring strangers into your group. That way, you and your friends get the opportunity to check out the new person together.

If you are out for an evening, try to stay with the group, particularly if it is dark. Sometimes, it is even dangerous for couples to separate from the group. I know this may sound silly, but criminals have occasionally targeted pairs of students.

3. **Avoid isolated and abandoned areas.** Stay away from rarely traveled routes, empty buildings, unused parks, shortcuts behind buildings, paths under bridges, or trails through the woods, and any other place that others rarely frequent.

4. **Notify others of changes in plans. If for some reason you must separate from the group, tell several people where you are going,** even if it is to the women's or the men's room. If you are attending a large sporting event or big nightclub, it is easy to get lost in a crowd. In the excitement of the evening, friends can easily lose track of group members. Stay in touch with the group throughout the day or evening. This is not paranoia, just safety. If you change plans and decide to leave early or arrive later, let someone know.

5. **Strangers plus cars can equal trouble. Hitchhiking is out of the question even if there are other people with you.** Yes, people are still doing that. **Be the exception. No hitchhiking!**

6. **Avoid meeting strangers off campus alone, even if it is broad daylight.** Find a way

to include them in the group.

7. Guard personal information carefully when using the Internet. Try to meet people through other people you know. If you do experiment with meeting someone on the Internet, do not give a home address, age, telephone numbers, or a daily schedule until you know more about this person. Again, find a way to meet strangers in a group of other students. If you receive an unsolicited email asking for personal information, delete it. There are thousands of scam artist looking for unsuspecting targets.

8. Be careful about giving your keys or locker combinations to other people. This includes keys to your home, dormitory, car, or locker. Another person may seem to be innocent and have honorable intentions while plotting against you, the unsuspecting student. So keep all keys and combinations to yourself and in a secure place. Many criminals know their victim, even if only through one meeting. That's how criminals get close enough to the victim to commit the crime. Criminals don't want their victims screaming, kicking, and making loud noises. That is why someone they know is a better target. **Make sure it is not you.**

9. Keep all bank and credit card information secure and private. Do not let others use your ATM card or credit card. Do not leave bank statements lying around for others to see. Protect your identifying information such as your driver's license and passport. You should develop a system now for handling and filing bank statements and credit card statements. What you do not file should be shredded. Students are prime targets for identify theft since they usually have clean credit records and no criminal history. Parents, resist the urge to handle these matters for your children. If they learn to handle their business affairs now, they will be so much more responsible later and much, much safer.

10. Don't leave doors open at home or in the dormitory for others to enter. Lock all doors. When your guest arrives and rings the bell, ask who it is and then, open the door. Home invasions occur in residential neighborhoods and in dormitories. Students in the dormitories have the habit of leaving secure doors open for guests to enter. Girls follow this practice to let in boys, and boys do the same for the girls. This is a bad practice. When the door is open, no one is secure.

11. Check out your neighborhood and college campus for emergency resources. Know where the police and fire stations are in your area. Know the telephone numbers of several neighbors. Check the campus for red help phones, usually located strategically around campus for students to access if needed.

12. Keep your cell phone charged and with you when you are away from home or out of the residence hall. Do not lend your cell phone to others. If you are too late getting home, others can seek you out by telephoning you, and if you don't answer, they can start looking for you.

None of these security measures is intended to frighten you or stifle your fun. Their purpose is to help ensure your safety at college and at home. Students who start practicing good safety habits in high school will find it easy to do in college without even thinking. You and your parents invested a lot of time, energy, money, and personal hope in your college admission and your future success. A few minutes spent taking simple precautions can go a long way to safeguarding a lifetime.

Best wishes for an awesome future.

VISIT THESE INTERNET SITES

www.commonapp.org Great resource for completing college applications.

www.collegevalues.org Great resource for finding colleges that emphasize character development and service.

www.thednaedge.com Great tool for self-discovery.

www.collegeandcharacter.org Lists colleges that encourage character development and service.

www.educationplanner.com Wonderful resource by American Education Services and supported by the Peterson's College Guide.

www.collegeboard.com Information about the PSAT, SAT, and other college related tests. Resource for college campus information and admissions policies.

www.collegedata.com Information about colleges and admission policies.

www.collegeview.com Interactive information about various colleges.

www.ecampustours.com If you can't go for a visit, this is the next best thing.

www.liu.edu/friendsworld Cross-cultural Education,Global Issues

www.bu.edu/education/caec Center for the Advancement of Ethics

www.quinnipiac.edu Albert Schweitzer Institute/ International programs for service.

www.mycollegeoptions.com More information about college admissions, easy to navigate.

www.collegeapps.about.com A good way to look for online applications on one site.

www.ed.gov/studentaid U.S. Department of Education's Web site. This is an excellent resource for all students. Definitely check this one out.

www.abetterchance.org Scholarships and other important resources for minority students.

www.ctaspira.org Scholarships for Latino students.

www.collegeboard.org A wealth of information about college scholarships, education research college entrance testing and more.

www.collegenet.com Good way to start your research.

www.fastweb.com One of my favorite scholarship search sites.

www.finaid.org Another great scholarship search site.

www.hsf.net Hispanic Scholarship Fund

www.hispanicfund.org Great resource with information about colleges and universities

www.heath.gwu.edu National Clearinghouse on post secondary education and financial aid for individuals with disabilities.

www.iefa.org Great data search for international students.

www.uncf.org/scholarship United Negro College Fund

www.wiredscholar.com Great resource for scholarships and colleges.

www.yahoo.com/education/financial_aid Great scholarship database. Thanks, Yahoo.

www.abfse.org/html/scholarship.html American Board of Funeral Service Scholarship.

www.bhpr.hrsa.gov/nursing/loanrepay.htm Nursing Education Loan Repayment Program Sponsored by the U.S. Department of Health and Human Services.

www.ed.gov/offices/OSFAP/Students/repayment/teachers Federal loan cancellation and/or deferment for teachers.

www.ffa.org Future Farmers of America

www.pdkintl.org. Phi Delta Kappa scholarships for prospective educators.

www.legion.org American Legion's Web site, which provides instructions for ordering their college financial aid handbook, Need a Lift.

www.military.com All branches of the military

www.va.gov U. S. Department of Veteran Affairs for veterans' educational benefits.

www.fsu.edu/staffair/institute Information about character and values in college.

www.naca.org National Association of Campus Activities.

STATE RESOURCES

Alabama

Alabama Commission on Higher Education

P.O. Box 302000

Montgomery, Alabama 36130

800-960-7773

334-242-1998

Alaska

State Department of Education

Goldbelt Place

801 West 10th Street, Suite 200

Juneau, Alaska 99801-1894

907-465-2884

Arizona

Arizona Commission of Postsecondary Education

2020 North Central Ave., Suite 275

Phoenix, Arizona 85004

602-229-2531

State Department of Education

1535 West Jefferson

Phoenix, Arizona 85007

602-542-2147

Arkansas

Arkansas Department of Higher Education

114 East Capitol

Little Rock, Arkansas 72201

501-371-2000

California

California Student Aid Commission

P.O. Box 419026

Rancho Cordova, CA 95741

916-526-7900

Colorado

Colorado Commission on Higher Education

Colorado Heritage Center

1300 Broadway, 2nd floor

Denver, Colorado 80203

303-866-2723

State Department of Education

201 East Colfax Avenue

Denver, Colorado 80203

303-866-6779

Connecticut

Connecticut Department of Higher Education

61 Woodland Street

Hartford, Connecticut 06105

860-947-1855, 800-842-0229

Connecticut Department of Education

165 Capitol Avenue

Hartford, Connecticut 06106

Delaware

Delaware Higher Education commission

Carvel State Office Building, fourth Floor

820 North French Street

Wilmington, Delaware 19801

302-577-3240

State Department of Public Instruction

Townsend Building #279

Federal and Lockerman Streets

Dover Delaware 19903

302-739-4583

District of Columbia

Department of Human Services

Office of Postsecondary Education

Research and Assistance

441 4th Street N.W.

Washington, D.C. 20001

202-727-6436

D.C. Tuition Assistance Grant

www.tuitiongrant.dc.gov

Florida

Florida Department of Education

Office of Student Financial Assistance

1940 North Monroe St. #70

Tallahassee, Florida 32303

850-410-5200

Georgia

Georgia Student Finance Commission

State Loans and Grants Division

Suite 245

2082 East Exchange Place

Tucker, Georgia 30334

770-724-9000

Hawaii

Hawaii State Postsecondary Education Commission

2444 Dole Street, Room 202

Honolulu, Hawaii 96822-2394

808-956-8213

Hawaii Department of Education

2530 10th Avenue, Room A12

Honolulu, Hawaii 96816

808-733-9103

Idaho

Idaho Board of Education

P.O. Box 83720

Boise, Idaho 83720-0037

208-334-2270

State Department of Education

650 West State Street

Boise, Idaho 83720

208-334-2113

Illinois

Illinois Student Assistance Commission

1755 Lake Cook Road

Deerfield, Illinois 60015-5209

847-948-8500

Indiana

State Student Assistance Commission of Indiana

Suite 500k, 150 West Market Street

Indianapolis, Indiana 46204-2811

317-232-2350

Iowa

Iowa College Student Aid Commission

914 Grand Avenue, Suite 201

Des Moines, Iowa 50309

800-383-4222

Kansas

Kansas Board of Regents

Student Financial Aid

1000 South West Jackson Street

Suite 520

Topeka Kansas 66612

785-296-3421

Kentucky

Kentucky Higher Education Assistance Authority

Suite 102, 1050 U.S. 127 South

Frankfort, Kentucky 40601-4323

800-928-8926

State Department of Education

500 Mero Street

1919 Capital Plaza Tower

Frankfort, Kentucky 40601

502-564-3421

Louisiana

Louisiana Student Financial Assistance Commission

Office of Student Financial Assistance

P.O. Box 91202

Baton Rouge, Louisiana 70821-9202

800-259-5626

Maine

Maine Department of Education

Office of Higher Education

23 State House Station

Augusta, Maine 04333-0023

207-624-6600

Maryland

Maryland Higher Education Commission

839 Bestgate Road, Suite 400

Annapolis, Maryland 21401

410-260-4500, 800-974-0203

Maryland State Department of Education

200 West Baltimore Street

Baltimore, Maryland 21201

410-767-0480

Massachusetts

Massachusetts Office of Student Financial Assistance

330 Stuart Street

Boston, Massachusetts 02116

617-727-9420

Massachusetts College Access Center

666 Boylston St.

Boston, Massachusetts 02116

617-536-0200

Michigan

Michigan Higher Education Assistance Authority

Office of Scholarships and Grants

P.O. Box 30462

Lansing, Michigan 48909

517-373-3394

Minnesota

Minnesota Office of Higher Education

Suite 400, Capitol Square Bldg.

550 Cedar Street

St. Paul, Minnesota 55101

800-657-3866

Mississippi

Mississippi Postsecondary Education

Student Financial Aid

3825 Ridgewood Road

Jackson, Mississippi 39211

601-432-6997

Missouri

Missouri Coordinating Board of Higher Education

3515 Amazonas Drive

Jefferson City, Missouri 65109

573-751-2361

Montana

Montana University System

Office of Higher Education

2500 Broadway

Helena, Montana 59620

406-444-6570

Nebraska

Coordinating Commission for Postsecondary Education

P.O. Box 95005

Lincoln, Nebraska 68509

402-471-2847

Nevada

Nevada Department of Education

700 E. 5th Street

Capitol Complex

Carson City, Nevada 89710

775-687-9200

New Hampshire

New Hampshire Postsecondary Education Commission

2 Industrial Park Drive

Concord, New Hampshire 03301

603-271-2555

New Jersey

State of New Jersey

Office of Student Financial assistance

4 Quakerbridge Plaza, CN540

Trenton, New Jersey 08625

800-792-8670

New Mexico

New Mexico Commission on Higher Education

1068 Cerrillos Road

Santa Fe, New Mexico 87501

505-827-7383

New York

New York State Higher Education Services Corporation

One Commerce Plaza

Albany, New York 12255

518-474-5642

North Carolina

North Carolina State Education Assistance Authority

www.cfnc.org

919-549-8614

North Carolina College Foundation

866-866-2362

North Dakota

North Dakota University System

North Dakota Student Financial Assistance Program

600 East Boulevard Avenue

Bismarck, North Dakota 58505

701-328-5835

Ohio

Ohio Board of Regents

State Grants and Scholarships

309 South 4th Street, Room 1005

Columbus, Ohio 43218

888-833-1133

Oklahoma

Oklahoma State Regents for Higher Education

Oklahoma Guaranteed Student Loan Program

P.O. Box 3000

Oklahoma City, Ok 73101

1-800-247-0420

Oregon

Oregon Student Assistance Commission

Suite 100, 1500 Valley River Drive

Eugene, Oregon 97401

541-687-7400

Pennsylvania

Pennsylvania Higher Education Assistance Agency

1200 North Seventh Street

Harrisburg, Pennsylvania 17102

717-720-2860

Rhode Island

Rhode Island Higher Education Assistance Authority

560 Jefferson Boulevard

Warwick, Rhode Island 02886

800-922-9855

South Carolina

South Carolina Higher Education Tuition Grants Commission

1310 Lady Street, Suite 811

P.O. Box 12159

Columbia, South Carolina 29201

803-896-1120

South Dakota

Department of Education and Cultural Affairs

Office of the Secretary

700 Governors Drive

'Pierre, South Dakota 57501

605-773-3134

Tennessee

Tennessee Higher Education Commission

404 James Robertson Parkway

Suite 1900

Nashville, Tennessee 37243

615-741-3605

Texas

Texas Higher Education Coordinating Board

P.O. Box 12788, Capitol Station

Austin, Texas 78711

800-242-3062

Utah

Utah State Board of Regents

Utah System of Higher Education

355 West North Temple

#3 Triad Center, Suite 550

Salt Lake City, Utah 84180

801-321-7100

Vermont

Vermont Student Assistance Corporation

Champlain Mill

P.O. Box 2000

Winooski, Vermont 05404

800-642-3177

Virginia

State Council of Higher Education for Virginia

James Monroe Building

101 North Fourteenth Street

Richmond, Virginia 23219

804-786-1690

Washington

Washington State Higher Education Coordinating Board

P.O. Box 43430

917 Lakeridge Way, S.W.

Olympia, Washington 98504

360-753-7800

West Virginia

State college and University Systems of West Virginia Central Office

Office of Financial Aid

1018 Kanawha Boulevard East, Suite 700

Charleston, West Virginia 25301

304-558-4614

Wisconsin

Higher Educational Aids Board

P.O. Box 7885

Madison, Wisconsin 53707

608-267-2206

Wyoming

Wyoming State Department of Education

Hathaway Building

2300 Capitol Avenue, 2nd Floor

Cheyenne, Wyoming 82002

307-777-6265

When you have finished your review of Internet resources, make a list of the Web addresses you want to contact and indicate actions required or deadline dates to remember.

Web addresses	Action	Deadline Dates
_____	_____	_____
_____	_____	_____
_____	_____	_____
_____	_____	_____
_____	_____	_____
_____	_____	_____
_____	_____	_____
_____	_____	_____
_____	_____	_____
_____	_____	_____

Recommended Reading

Colleges That Change Lives: 40 schools you should know about even if you're not a straight A student. Author, Loren Pope (Penguin Books, 2000)

Colleges That Encourage Character Development, Edited by the John Templeton Foundation (Templeton Foundation Press, 1999)

The DNA of Successful Leaders. Troy L. Tate (Cumulatius Publishing, 2006) Be sure to take the personality profile. You can do it on line.

Making a Life, Making a Living: Reclaiming Your Purpose and Passion in Business and In Life. Mark Albion. (Warner Books, 2000) The millionaire study is on page 17.

Our Endangered Values: America's Moral Crisis by Jimmy Carter (Simon & Schuster, 2005)

I want to hear your comments and your success stories as you go through the college admissions process. I'd love to hear about the colleges you enter, how you made your choice, and how you financed your education. When you find your purpose, I'd like to hear about that too.

Contact me at **www. Achievementworks.com**

Carolynbaker@achievementworks.com

ABOUT THE AUTHOR

Carolyn Croom Baker started her college placement career in Washington, D.C. working with students planning for careers in the arts. Her students discovered that anyone who desires a college education and who is willing to invest in his or her goals can attend one of America's best colleges and secure all of the necessary financing. From that time, her constant passion has been college access for all students. The decision to attend or not belongs to the family, but at minimum, access is essential. Carolyn Baker has helped over 5,000 students make their dreams of a college education real.

Carolyn later moved to Connecticut where she has served as a school district coordinator of guidance services, guidance counselor, adjunct instructor at Southern Connecticut State University in the Graduate Department of Counseling and School Psychology, Director of Education for the Albert Schweitzer Institute and co-coordinator of the Aspirations for Higher Learning Pre-College Programs. Carolyn has presented her views on college access, college placement, and service learning at local and regional conferences including the New England Regional Meeting of the College Board.

Carolyn Croom Baker

Currently, Carolyn provides college placement services to groups and families, continues public speaking engagements, and writes frequently on the subject. Her latest venture, Achievement Works provides additional information, training, and support to new counseling professionals, organizations involved with first generation college attendees, parents, and students about college placement and college access.

Carolyn Croom Baker is a member of the American Counseling Association and is a National Certified Counselor. She resides in Connecticut.

Printed in the United States
87229LV00010B/13-90/A

9 781421 899169